MW01591701

National Guard Youth ChalleNGe and Job ChalleNGe

Metrics for Success

STEPHANI L. WRABEL, JOSHUA EAGAN, GRACE FALGOUST,
JENNA W. KRAMER, JACK KROGER, JONAH KUSHNER,
KATA MIHALY, PETER NGUYEN, THOMAS E. TRAIL,
JENNIE W. WENGER, ERIK C. NESS

Prepared for the Office of the Secretary of Defense
Approved for public release; distribution is unlimited.

NATIONAL DEFENSE RESEARCH INSTITUTE

For more information on this publication, visit **www.rand.org/t/RRA1229-3**.

About RAND

RAND is a research organization that develops solutions to public policy challenges to help make communities throughout the world safer and more secure, healthier and more prosperous. RAND is nonprofit, nonpartisan, and committed to the public interest. To learn more about RAND, visit www.rand.org.

Research Integrity

Our mission to help improve policy and decisionmaking through research and analysis is enabled through our core values of quality and objectivity and our unwavering commitment to the highest level of integrity and ethical behavior. To help ensure our research and analysis are rigorous, objective, and nonpartisan, we subject our research publications to a robust and exacting quality-assurance process; avoid both the appearance and reality of financial and other conflicts of interest through staff training, project screening, and a policy of mandatory disclosure; and pursue transparency in our research engagements through our commitment to the open publication of our research findings and recommendations, disclosure of the source of funding of published research, and policies to ensure intellectual independence. For more information, visit www.rand.org/about/research-integrity.

RAND's publications do not necessarily reflect the opinions of its research clients and sponsors.

Published by the RAND Corporation, Santa Monica, Calif.
© 2024 RAND Corporation
RAND® is a registered trademark.

Library of Congress Cataloging-in-Publication Data is available for this publication.

ISBN: 978-1-9774-1316-1

Cover: Crystal Housman/U.S. Air National Guard.

Limited Print and Electronic Distribution Rights

This publication and trademark(s) contained herein are protected by law. This representation of RAND intellectual property is provided for noncommercial use only. Unauthorized posting of this publication online is prohibited; linking directly to its webpage on rand.org is encouraged. Permission is required from RAND to reproduce, or reuse in another form, any of its research products for commercial purposes. For information on reprint and reuse permissions, please visit www.rand.org/pubs/permissions.

About This Report

The National Guard Youth ChalleNGe (Youth ChalleNGe) program is a residential, quasi-military program for young people aged 16–18 who are at risk of not completing high school. Job ChalleNGe, offered to Youth ChalleNGe graduates, focuses on providing in-depth job training and workplace acculturation. RAND has been conducting research on these programs since 2016 and has amassed data and insights about program operations, challenges, and successes. Most of our prior research relied on information provided by ChalleNGe staff and through cadet data files, interviews, and site visits. In this report, we expand on our work by integrating the perspective of Job ChalleNGe participants and leveraging external statewide education and labor administrative data. These analyses provide new insights for ChalleNGe leadership and individual sites to use in their decisionmaking.

The research reported here was completed in March 2024 and underwent security review with the sponsor and the Defense Office of Prepublication and Security Review before public release.

RAND National Security Research Division

This research was sponsored by the Office of the Assistant Secretary of Defense for Manpower and Reserve Affairs and conducted within the Personnel, Readiness, and Health Program of the RAND National Security Research Division (NSRD), which operates the National Defense Research Institute (NDRI), a federally funded research and development center sponsored by the Office of the Secretary of Defense, the Joint Staff, the Unified Combatant Commands, the Navy, the Marine Corps, the defense agencies, and the defense intelligence enterprise.

For more information on the RAND Personnel, Readiness, and Health Program, see www.rand.org/nsrd/prh or contact the director (contact information is provided on the webpage).

Acknowledgments

We want to thank the many individuals who contributed their time and expertise that enhanced the quality of this report, including Michelle Bongard, Robert Bozick, Louay Constant, Linda Cottrell, Sy Doan, Joy Moini, and James Murphy. Holly Kosiewicz and Isaiah Simmons helped improve this research through their constructive reviews. We recognize the support of our editors and publications team, including Fadia Afashe. Any flaws that remain are solely the authors' responsibility.

We appreciate the staff in the Georgia Governor's Office of Student Achievement, who engaged in many conversations about their data systems and conducted linking procedures with data from the ChalleNGe program. We thank ChalleNGe leaders in Georgia for providing the Governor's Office of Student Achievement with data that made our analyses possible. We thank the leadership and participants of the six Job ChalleNGe sites who welcomed us to their campuses and shared their perspectives in our focus groups. Finally, we thank our action officer, Michael J. O'Toole, for his investment in and support of our research.

The contents of this report were developed using data provided by Georgia's Academic and Workforce Analysis and Research Data System (GA•AWARDS). However, those contents do not necessarily represent the policy of GA•AWARDS or any of its participating organizations, and you should not assume endorsement by GA•AWARDS or any of its participating organizations.

Summary

The National Guard Youth ChalleNGe (Youth ChalleNGe) Program is a residential, quasi-military program for young people aged 16–18 who are at risk of not completing high school; the program's stated mission is to "intervene in and reclaim the lives of at-risk youth and produce program graduates with the values, skills, education, and self-discipline necessary to succeed as adults" (National Guard Youth ChalleNGe Program, 2015, p. 2).[1] Over its more-than-30-year history, Youth ChalleNGe has expanded from a pilot program with ten sites to a well-established program with 40 sites and more than 200,000 graduates. Job ChalleNGe, originally established as a three-site pilot program in 2016, is modeled after Youth ChalleNGe but has a focus on providing in-depth job training to some Youth ChalleNGe graduates. As of October 2023, there were six Job ChalleNGe sites, with two additional sites planned to begin operations over the next two years. Both Youth and Job ChalleNGe sites operate through their state National Guard organizations; the National Guard Bureau is responsible for daily operations, while the Office of the Secretary of Defense provides policy guidance and broad oversight.

Focus of This Report and Description of Project Tasks

Over the past eight years, RAND researchers have worked closely with ChalleNGe policymakers and program staff; as part of two overlapping projects, the RAND team has collected and reported data from all Youth ChalleNGe sites over 14 ChalleNGe classes, covering Youth ChalleNGe cadets who entered the program between 2015 and 2021. Over the same period, the RAND team has designed and carried out a variety of analytic efforts focused on Youth ChalleNGe and Job ChalleNGe.

This capstone report is the culmination of research and analyses conducted as part of RAND's second ChalleNGe research project, initially funded in 2019.[2] The project included three main tasks:

- collecting detailed data on a yearly basis from each Youth ChalleNGe site and using the data to produce analysis that forms the basis of the yearly annual report to Congress (as part of this project, the RAND team completed three annual reports covering the six classes that entered ChalleNGe in 2019–2021) (Wenger et al., 2021; Wenger, Constant, et al., 2022; Wenger, Cottrell, and Wrabel, 2023)

---

[1] At times, programs admit young people who will turn 16 or 19 during their time in the program.

[2] A similar capstone report (Wenger, Wrabel, et al., 2022) documents analyses carried out as part of the first RAND project on ChalleNGe.

- designing and conducting two different studies to improve the effectiveness of the Job ChalleNGe program (which is still in its first decade): the first, a process/implementation study, which included the collection of qualitative and quantitative data with a goal of understanding several aspects of the program: differences in delivery, strengths and weaknesses, and barriers and facilitators; and the second, an outcomes study, which tested different methods of measuring participant outcomes
- collecting and analyzing data for small pilot projects occurring within one or more program sites.

In this report, we summarize some of the results of the first task (more details can be found in the annual reports); we also provide detailed information on the results of the second task. The results of the pilot projects are reported in other documents.[3]

Data Sources and Methodologies Employed

We report on four streams of analysis in this report that served to address our two research tasks. First, we use yearly data provided by Youth ChalleNGe sites to describe programwide trends over the past seven years (2015–2021); we focus on enrollment and graduation trends. We also conducted a series of analyses, using Youth ChalleNGe cadet data and external data sources, to understand whom Youth ChalleNGe serves and the communities from which these individuals are drawn. We gathered additional data on Job ChalleNGe implementation; to do this, we used a short survey, discussions with staff, and focus groups with participants. These results build on previously reported analyses (see Wenger, Constant, et al., 2022). Previous analyses used a variety of data sources, but this is the first time we have been able to include participants' perspectives, gathered through focus groups held at each of the six Job ChalleNGe sites. Finally, we secured access to the State Longitudinal Data System in Georgia, in which kindergarten through 12th grade (K–12) education, postsecondary education, and labor market data were merged with Youth and Job ChalleNGe participant data, to conduct a proof-of-concept analysis on long-term outcomes.

Key Findings

Consistent with their mission, Youth and Job ChalleNGe programs serve young people from disadvantaged communities. Even within program participants, there are differences by race and ethnicity; Black and Latino participants come from less advantaged communities. This result holds when we compare communities on traditional economic measures (such as income, education, and unemployment) and when we compare social networks within communities.

---

[3] See Corte and Sontag-Padilla, 2021; Constant et al., 2021; Edwards, Zaber, and Schwam, 2022, as well as the results of value-added models discussed in Wenger, Constant, et al., 2022.

This suggests that some participants may be less prepared when they arrive at ChalleNGe programs and that they may lack social ties that often lead to employment.

Job ChalleNGe sites provide a wide array of resources, supports, and services to participants, but resources available through educational or training partners, such as supplemental academic support and physical/mental health services, are used less often. Job ChalleNGe staff are committed to providing educational and job training opportunities to participants and ensuring that participants find productive opportunities, but the sites have not yet begun to fully utilize the additional supports available through their training partners.

In focus groups, Job ChalleNGe participants reported an appreciation of the opportunities offered by the program. *Participants also reported misalignment between the initial description of the program and their lived experiences.* Relevant discussions often focused on policies about home visits and the use of electronic devices. This perceived misalignment has led to frustration and some dissatisfaction. It is not surprising that participants' experiences with homesickness and limited opportunities to communicate with family and friends also played a role here. But participants also reported that staff shortages had negatively affected some of their experiences.

We leveraged data from Georgia as a proof-of-concept measurement of long-term outcomes for Youth and Job ChalleNGe program graduates. Although the analysis had substantial limitations, it also provided several insights. *Georgia Youth and Job ChalleNGe participants were more likely than similar young people to complete postsecondary certifications and to hold a job.* The effects on annual wages were mixed; this could be driven by differences in continued enrollment in education and training programs, hours worked, or types of jobs.

Over the course of two projects, the RAND team has systematically explored options for collecting and assessing ChalleNGe participants' long-term outcomes. Primary approaches include maintaining contact with each graduate, periodically surveying graduates, and matching graduates to state or national existing data systems (see Wenger, Wrabel, Trail, et al., 2022). During the course of this project, we tested the option of accessing one state's data system to track (Youth and Job) ChalleNGe participants' outcomes. *While matching participant information to a state's data system provided useful information, this option is likely not practical for most or all sites.* This is due to the administrative burdens and the time lags involved. A centralized effort, using a national administrative database or surveying a representative sample of participants, appears more practical.

Recommendations

Cadets from the most poorly resourced communities may require additional supports after leaving ChalleNGe. Our analyses demonstrate that many cadets come from communities with relatively low levels of education, income, and economic connectedness, and that cadets from historically marginalized racial and ethnic groups come from communities that are more disadvantaged than those of their peers. As the program is currently designed, cadet mentors provide most post-residential support; mentors also help to connect graduates with employment opportunities. ChalleNGe may need to consider how it structures and resources the post-residential phase to ensure all graduates are connecting with opportunities. To the extent that program staff have developed specific strategies to provide additional support, we recommend information-sharing, as well as test cases or pilot projects, in this area. The long-term success of Youth and Job ChalleNGe participants, and of the programs more broadly, is heavily dependent on graduates being able to identify opportunities during the post-residential phase of the program.

Staff should more fully utilize the resources and services available through their educational partners. Partners frequently offer academic supports and help with career development, as well as physical and mental health services. The Job ChalleNGe program staff have worked hard to develop a wide variety of supports and activities for participants, but additional resources available from their educational partners could help alleviate some of the pressures on Job ChalleNGe to offer more comprehensive health and employment services.

In the wake of the coronavirus disease 2019 pandemic, many participants of Youth ChalleNGe will be interested in learning more about Job ChalleNGe. *We recommend, based on analyses of participants' perspectives, that sites carefully calibrate the information provided to potential Job ChalleNGe participants; experiences conveyed should accurately represent the details of credentials and certifications, as well as the lived experiences of participants through details about the living arrangements and program's structure.* Providing consistent messaging helps establish accurate expectations for future Job ChalleNGe participants and may generate additional program satisfaction among participants. At times, the current messaging is not sufficiently aligned with participants' experiences. Developing common recruiting materials that can be used across sites and stakeholder groups may be helpful.

Although measuring long-term outcomes of program participants is especially difficult in a multisite program in which participants return to communities across the United States, such information remains key to determining overall program effectiveness. *To this end, we recommend piloting a central effort to survey graduates.* In this report and in our earlier reports, we provide more details about the pros and cons of different options to collect this information. The option for collecting long-term outcomes that appears most promising as of this writing is to link ChalleNGe data with existing national datasets or use external (centrally administered) surveys, including a complete sampling and a strategic or representative sampling of graduates. A central administrative database for the ChalleNGe programs could play a key role in this strategy. Because of the overlapping time frames of our ChalleNGe projects, the RAND team is already testing these options to provide the U.S. Department of Defense with additional insights on how to best measure long-term outcomes of the Youth and Job ChalleNGe programs.

Contents

About This Report.. iii

Summary v

Figures and Tables xi

CHAPTER 1

Introduction and Background.. 1

    Overview of Youth ChalleNGe and Job ChalleNGe.. 2

    RAND's ChalleNGe Research 6

    Contribution and Organization of This Report 8

CHAPTER 2

Youth ChalleNGe Participants and Their Home Communities... 9

    Trends in the U.S. Youth Population 9

    Describing Youth ChalleNGe Cadets' Communities 11

    Limitations.. 17

    Conclusion.. 18

CHAPTER 3

Job ChalleNGe Implementation.. 19

    Prior Job ChalleNGe Findings and Study Contribution.. 20

    Data and Methods 20

    Program Implementation Findings.. 25

    Conclusion.. 41

CHAPTER 4

Long-Term Outcomes for Youth and Job ChalleNGe Graduates in Georgia......................... 43

    Analysis Overview... 44

    Results 53

    Limitations.. 65

    Conclusion.. 66

CHAPTER 5

Summary and Recommendations.. 69

    Summary of Key Findings 70

    Recommendations 71

    Areas for Future Research 74

APPENDIXES

A. Additional Information About Neighborhood Analyses..77

B. Long-Term Outcome Supplemental Materials 89
C. Survey Development and Administration 105

Abbreviations 113
References 115

Figures and Tables

Figures

1.1.   Youth ChalleNGe Logic Model 7
2.1.   Differences in Youth ChalleNGe Cadets' Neighborhoods and U.S. Average
        Levels of Economic Hardship 14
2.2.   Differences in Youth ChalleNGe Cadets' Neighborhoods, by Race
        and Ethnicity 16
4.1.   Demographic Characteristics of Youth and Job ChalleNGe Graduates
        Compared with Students in Georgia 54
4.2.   Absences and Disciplinary Outcomes of Youth and Job ChalleNGe Graduates
        Compared with Students in Georgia 55
4.3.   Academic Achievement of Youth and Job ChalleNGe Graduates Compared
        with Students in Georgia 56
4.4.   Enrollment in Two-Year Institution of Youth and Job ChalleNGe Graduates
        Compared with Students in Georgia 59
4.5.   Postsecondary Credentials of Youth and Job ChalleNGe Graduates Compared
        with Students in Georgia 60
4.6.   Labor Force Participation of Youth and Job ChalleNGe Graduates Compared
        with Students in Georgia 61
4.7.   Annual Wages of Youth and Job ChalleNGe Graduates Compared with
        Students in Georgia 62
4.8.   Impact of Youth ChalleNGe on Enrollment in a Two-Year Institution 63
4.9.   Impact of Youth ChalleNGe on Postsecondary Credentials 63
4.10.   Impact of Youth ChalleNGe on Labor Force Participation 64
4.11.   Impact of Youth ChalleNGe on Annual Wages 65
B.1.   Effect Size Difference Before and After Propensity Score Weighting,
        Education Outcomes, Within Five Years 97
B.2.   Effect Size Difference Before and After Propensity Score Weighting,
        Education Outcomes, Within Six Years 98
B.3.   Effect Size Difference Before and After Propensity Score Weighting,
        Education Outcomes, Within Seven Years 98
B.4.   Effect Size Difference Before and After Propensity Score Weighting,
        Education Outcomes, Within Eight Years 99
B.5.   Effect Size Difference Before and After Propensity Score Weighting,
        Labor Force Participation, All Years 99
B.6.   Effect Size Difference Before and After Propensity Score Weighting,
        Annual Wages, Age 17–18 100
B.7.   Effect Size Difference Before and After Propensity Score Weighting,
        Annual Wages, Age 18–19 100
B.8.   Effect Size Difference Before and After Propensity Score Weighting,
        Annual Wages, Age 19–20 101
B.9.   Effect Size Difference Before and After Propensity Score Weighting,
        Annual Wages, Age 20–21 101

B.10. Effect Size Difference Before and After Propensity Score Weighting, Annual Wages, Age 21–22 102
B.11. Effect Size Difference Before and After Propensity Score Weighting, Total Earnings, All Ages 102

Tables

3.1. Number of Interviews and Focus Groups, by Site 22
3.2. Demographic Characteristics of Job ChalleNGe Focus Group Participants, Aggregated Across Sites 23
3.3. Job ChalleNGe Training Program and Post-Program Plans Among Focus Group Participants, Aggregated Across Sites 24
3.4. Number of Sites Leveraging Education Partners, by Service and Resource 39
4.1. Cohorts of 8th-Grade Students Across School Years in the Analysis File 48
4.2. Education Outcomes and 8th-Grade Cohorts 49
4.3. Number of Youth and Job ChalleNGe Graduates in Georgia, by School Year 51
4.4. Sample Sizes for Background Characteristics 51
4.5. Education Outcomes, Cohorts and Sample Sizes 52
4.6. Labor Force Outcomes and Sample Sizes 52
4.7. Youth and Job ChalleNGe Graduate Postsecondary Enrollment and Attainment 57
4.8. Youth and Job ChalleNGe Graduate Labor Market Outcomes 58
A.1. Economic and Social Measures: Youth ChalleNGe Cadets Versus Benchmark U.S. Zip Codes 79
A.2. Economic and Social Measures: Mean Differences Between Youth ChalleNGe and Non–Youth ChalleNGe Zip Codes 81
A.3. Differences in Youth ChalleNGe Cadet Social Capital Outcomes, by Race and Ethnicity and Gender 82
A.4. Differences in Youth ChalleNGe Cadet Demographics, by Race and Ethnicity and Gender 83
A.5. Differences in Youth ChalleNGe Cadet Poverty and Income, by Race and Ethnicity and Gender 84
A.6. Differences in Youth ChalleNGe Cadet Labor Force Outcomes, by Race and Ethnicity and Gender 85
A.7. Youth ChalleNGe Cadets Compared with U.S. Average and Robustness Checks for Non-Pandemic Years and Only Youth ChalleNGe Graduates 87
B.1. Average Characteristics of Schools With and Without Youth ChalleNGe Participants, Compared with All Schools in Georgia 93
B.2. Student Demographics 94
B.3. Absence and Discipline 94
B.4. Standardized Test Scores 94
B.5. Credentials 95
B.6. Enrollment in Two-Year Institution 95
B.7. Annual Wages 96
B.8. Total Earnings 96

B.9.   Labor Force Participation 96
B.10.   Coefficient Estimates, Standard Errors, and Sample Sizes, Impact of Youth
        ChalleNGe 103
C.1.   Count of Pre-Post Survey Invitations and Completions, by Site and
        Administration 109
C.2.   Count of Long-Term Outcomes Survey Invitations and Completions, by Site
        and Administration 109

CHAPTER 1

Introduction and Background

The National Guard Youth ChalleNGe (Youth ChalleNGe) program was established in 1993 as a pilot program to support communities in countering conflicting trends in the U.S. labor market and education. Well-paying, blue-collar jobs were being moved overseas, and new jobs often required increasing levels of educational credentials (Autor, 2014). Simultaneously, the high school dropout rate in the United States remained persistently high. Therefore, Youth ChalleNGe was established to "intervene in and reclaim the lives of at-risk youth and produce program graduates with the values, skills, education, and self-discipline necessary to succeed as adults" (National Guard Youth ChalleNGe Program, 2015, p. 2).[1] In 2016, to support ongoing job skill development and further the success of Youth ChalleNGe graduates, the Job ChalleNGe program was established as a three-site pilot program. As of February 2024, Youth ChalleNGe operates 39 sites in 30 states (including the District of Columbia and Puerto Rico), and there are six Job ChalleNGe sites, with two additional sites planned to begin operations over the next two years. ChalleNGe sites operate through their state National Guard organizations with supporting funds and oversight provided by the U.S. Department of Defense (DoD). An in-depth description of both programs is provided later in this chapter.

Over the past eight years, RAND researchers have worked closely with ChalleNGe policymakers and program staff as part of two overlapping projects. The RAND team has collected and reported on data from all Youth ChalleNGe sites over 14 ChalleNGe classes, covering Youth ChalleNGe participants who entered the program between 2015 and 2021.[2] Youth ChalleNGe sites maintain records on the numbers of applicants, entrants, and graduates and information describing the participants (such as age, gender, and height and weight). The sites also track participants' academic assessment scores and reports of their post-ChalleNGe activities; the data also include key aspects of each site's operation (such as the number of staff in key positions, starting salaries, total budget, and detail on some of the site-level policies). As a newer program, Job ChalleNGe has fewer historical records, but each site maintains information about participants. These data allow sites to meet their reporting requirements, but program sites lack the capacity to carry out detailed analyses using these data.

---

[1] The program includes youth aged 16–18 years but, at times, sites admit young people who will turn 16 or 19 during their time in the program. The program has also extended its focus to include young people who are at risk of dropping out rather than individuals who have already dropped out of the education system.

[2] The RAND team is under contract for a third project to collect data on participants through 2024.

RAND has used available program data to describe programwide trends for Youth ChalleNGe over the past eight years (2016–2023) and to describe the young people served by the program. We have also extended data collection to report on wider aspects of the Youth and Job ChalleNGe programs. This report is the culmination of research, initially funded in 2019, that revolved around three main tasks:

- Collect detailed data on a yearly basis from each Youth ChalleNGe site and analyze the data to produce three annual reports to Congress (2019–2021). Wenger, Cottrell, and Wrabel (2023) is an example of such reports.
- Design and conduct two studies of the Job ChalleNGe programs. The first study, a process/implementation study, included the collection of qualitative and quantitative data with a goal of understanding several aspects of the program: differences in delivery, strengths and weaknesses, and barriers and facilitators. The second study, an outcomes study, tested different methods of measuring participant outcomes. Both studies were designed to improve the effectiveness of the Job ChalleNGe program, which is still in its first decade.
- Collect and analyze data for small pilot projects occurring within one or more program sites. These include analyses of goal-setting practices, the provision of career and technical education (CTE), and skills needed for high-quality jobs.[3]

In this report, we (1) extend our analyses of Youth ChalleNGe data to assess ChalleNGe's alignment with its mission to serve at-risk youth, (2) present the second installment of analyses on Job ChalleNGe implementation, and (3) present our analyses of long-term outcomes for both Youth and Job ChalleNGe graduates. In the remainder of this chapter, we provide an overview of both Youth ChalleNGe and Job ChalleNGe, as well as a brief summary of RAND's ChalleNGe research to date and the contributions this report makes to our broader body of work.

Overview of Youth ChalleNGe and Job ChalleNGe

Originally established in 1993 with ten sites, Youth ChalleNGe was designed as a "whole person" intervention to address the multifaceted needs of disengaged young people (Price, 2010). The program was originally intended to take place on a military base; the quasi-military nature of the program was viewed as a key distinguishing characteristic since the program's founding, and the structure was seen as providing a counterbalance to the disengagement observed among young people.[4] Participants attend Youth ChalleNGe at no cost

---

[3] See Corte and Sontag-Padilla, 2021; Constant et al., 2021; and Edwards, Zaber, and Schwam, 2022, as well as the results of value-added models discussed in Wenger, Constant, et al., 2022.

[4] Today, many—but not all—sites are on military installations.

to them or their families. Each Youth ChalleNGe site operates two residential classes a year, which typically start in January and July.

The program includes a five-and-a-half-month residential phase followed by a 12-month post-residential phase. The residential phase begins with pre-ChalleNGe (also known as the *acclimation phase*) where participants, who voluntarily attend the program, are familiarized with the structures, routines, and expectations the program uses to instill success in participants. For example, cadets are taught basic military drill, participate in team-building exercises, and complete assessments used to place them into appropriate classes for academic instruction. In the remainder of the residential phase, the program focuses on eight core components: academic excellence, leadership and followership, responsible citizenship, service to community, life coping skills, physical fitness, health and hygiene, and job skills.

Consistent with the original design and regardless of specific site or location, the Youth ChalleNGe program typically includes certain aspects of military life, such as uniform clothing and open-bay sleeping quarters. Participants, generally referred to as *cadets*, are divided into platoons; some staff members, referred to as *cadre*, work with and monitor cadets around the clock.[5] Days include four to six hours in an intensive classroom setting and time for physical fitness activities, eating, studying, volunteering, and taking part in other planned activities. *Instructors*, some of whom are state-certified teachers, provide the academic instruction portion of the program to cadets. Each site establishes its own educational program. Some sites operate a state- or regionally authorized charter school, some provide credit recovery options through online education platforms, others focus on preparing students for a high school equivalency assessment (e.g., General Educational Development [GED] test), and others offer a mix of educational offerings. A site's educational offerings are often shaped by state-level education policies.

After program completion, graduates are expected to continue their education, enter the labor market, provide service to the community, or seek other productive pathways into adulthood. Most graduates return to their home community after program completion. Mentors, often a member of the graduate's home community, support these young people in their transition out of the residential phase and through the 12-month post-residential phase of the program. During the residential phase, cadets work through a Post-Residential Action Plan (P-RAP), which is a goal-setting instrument that helps cadets prepare for life as a Youth ChalleNGe graduate and plan, often with support from their mentor, the steps needed to meet their personal goals (see Corte and Sontag-Padilla, 2021, for more details).

As of this writing, nearly half a million young people have applied to enter a Youth ChalleNGe program, and nearly 275,000 have entered the program. More than 200,000 have

---

[5] Youth ChalleNGe participants are referred to as *cadets* only after completing an acclimation period during the first two weeks. For simplicity, we refer to participants as *cadets* when discussing Youth ChalleNGe. We reserve the term *participants* for Job ChalleNGe because the sites do not have a standard name for participating individuals. We also use *participants* when referencing the individuals at both Youth and Job ChalleNGe.

graduated from a Youth ChalleNGe program site.[6] Those who participate in the program go on to have higher levels of educational attainment and annual earnings than similar non-participants; moreover, the program is cost-effective and returns roughly $2.66 for each $1 invested.[7] In the years immediately preceding the coronavirus disease 2019 (COVID-19) pandemic, more than 12,000 young people typically entered the program, and roughly 10,000 graduated. The numbers of participants and graduates fell during the pandemic but have increased in each class since the end of 2020. Prior to the pandemic, 165–170 young people entered a typical site during each class (recall that there are two classes per year), and a typical site had a staff of about 65 people. Of course, variation exists in the program size of each site, and the number of operational sites has varied over time as well.[8]

Job ChalleNGe also typically lasts up to 22 weeks and is offered at no cost to participants and their families. Each Job ChalleNGe site operates two residential phases each year. Job ChalleNGe is also operated on military installations; participants live in bay-style housing and engage in activities aligned with the eight core components of the ChalleNGe model. The program, which is available only to Youth ChalleNGe graduates, emphasizes the job skills core component, providing in-depth job training and workplace acculturation. Participants have the opportunity to continue their academic study or participate in CTE training through college coursework or industry training. Training is offered largely in partnership with community colleges, although some sites also work with adult education centers or private companies that offer job training credentials. Participants select from CTE training tracks, such as automotive, construction, culinary arts, heavy equipment operator, information technology, phlebotomy, and welding.

Job ChalleNGe CTE training can lead to industry certificates and college credits, which both promote job placement and future financial stability. Program offerings are aligned with high-demand occupations in the region in which the program is located, and sites offer participants support in finding professional or educational placement after completion of the program. Job ChalleNGe, like its Youth ChalleNGe precursor, is intended to give its partici-

---

[6] We use *program* to refer to the entire ChalleNGe program; we use *site* to refer to one single location of the program. Several states have multiple Youth ChalleNGe sites. For additional background information, see Wenger, Cottrell, and Wrabel, 2023.

[7] Through a carefully designed randomized controlled trial using a subset of Youth ChalleNGe sites, researchers found that Youth ChalleNGe participants had higher levels of educational attainment and earnings (see Millenky et al., 2011; for calculations of cost-effectiveness, see Perez-Arce et al., 2012). It is worth noting that this study focused on a subset of Youth ChalleNGe sites and that the data were collected roughly 15 years ago.

[8] Our previous analyses indicated that size is an important driver of per-graduate costs and that sites with fewer than 75 graduates per class (150 graduates per year) tend to have higher costs than sites with more graduates (Wenger et al., 2017). During 2021, 22 sites fell below this cutoff. Five of the 22 sites did not operate for at least one class. We expect that the number of graduates will continue to increase over the next few years; this change will likely be reflected in lower per-graduate costs after adjusting for inflation.

pants, who experienced difficulty in traditional high school settings, access to a high-quality educational program in a stable, structured residential environment.

Youth ChalleNGe and Job ChalleNGe operate on well-defined models (see Price, 2010), but both programs also exist in wider ecosystems. In other words, the programs are affected by and often respond to key characteristics of the communities and states in which they are located, as well as relevant national trends. For example, Job ChalleNGe sites attempt to ensure that the job training they offer is aligned with jobs available and growth industries in their state. Youth ChalleNGe exists within a larger framework of educational programs (including other alternative programs); the options outside traditional public high schools vary widely by state. Youth ChalleNGe also emphasizes different credentials today than at its inception. The program was designed during a period when policymakers were focused on the dropout crisis; in the early 1990s, the dropout rate was more than twice what it is today, and passing the GED test was viewed as roughly equivalent to earning a high school diploma.[9] Thus, Youth ChalleNGe was designed as a program with a focus on passing the GED test. Over time, Youth ChalleNGe sites have increasingly offered options for credit recovery; some sites also award high school diplomas to cadets who meet all requirements. Shifts in the credentials offered and other changes in the education and labor market landscape have influenced activities at sites, but the Youth ChalleNGe model has remained consistent over the program's more-than-30-year history. Job ChalleNGe was designed more recently; its focus on occupation-specific training has been consistent throughout the program's relatively short life.

While Youth and Job ChalleNGe focus on improving participants' individual outcomes, the programs' focus on service, citizenship, and leadership and followership also positions ChalleNGe to have a positive effect in the broader communities served. In this way, ChalleNGe operates similarly to DoD's other predominant youth programs, STARBASE and Junior Reserve Officers' Training Corps; all three provide service to communities and seek to build a broader shared culture between the military and civilians. These programs are not recruiting tools for the military, but they may serve to introduce community members to the benefits of military service and thus are well positioned to help bridge the civilian-military divide.[10]

---

[9] Different calculations of the dropout rate exist, but the sharp decrease is present regardless of how the rate is measured (see de Brey, Zhang, and Duffy, 2022, Table 218.10). See Cameron and Heckman, 1993, for the initial documentation of key differences in outcomes between high school diploma graduates and those who earn a GED.

[10] STARBASE engages 5th-grade students in hands-on STEM instruction; Junior Reserve Officers' Training Corps serves high school students through a curriculum that emphasizes civic development and fitness and military history; see Wrabel et al. (2024) for more details on each program and about the ways in which these programs contribute to bridging the civilian-military divide. While Job ChalleNGe's mission is more focused on job training, this program may also have a positive influence in the communities served. Due to Job ChalleNGe's relatively short history and small footprint, no research to date has explored the impact of Job ChalleNGe on the civilian-military divide.

RAND's ChalleNGe Research

One aspect of RAND's work for this project includes providing an annual report to ChalleNGe leadership on the program's operations. These reports include descriptive information on the total numbers of applicants, participants, and graduates.[11] Reports also document the number of sites operating during each period and include detailed information on cadets' progress in terms of academic credentials, standardized test scores, and physical fitness. The reports track the hours of community service performed and the value of those hours; they document voter registration and Selective Service representation among eligible graduates. Starting with the 2020 data, the reports provide detailed information about the sites' response to the COVID-19 pandemic.

The reports include additional analyses of various site-level policies and practices. One consistent focus is on the relationships between cadet graduation rates, staff turnover, starting pay for ChalleNGe staff, and local labor market conditions. The reports document a clear relationship between these measures: Graduation rates are lower at sites with higher staff turnover, and turnover is higher and hiring is more difficult at sites with lower starting wages and higher local wages (Wenger, Constant, et al., 2021; Wenger, Cottrell, and Wrabel, 2023).

At the beginning of the first RAND ChalleNGe project, the research team developed a logic model as a tool to describe how the program's resources and activities would be expected to produce key outcomes and meet program goals. We have used the model to better understand and communicate the design of the ChalleNGe program. The model, which we have refined over time, appears in each annual report. Figure 1.1 shows the current version of the logic model.

Briefly, program inputs (or the resources needed to operate the program) include assets necessary to house and instruct participants, as well as policy and planning materials. Program activities are described in the model and include activities during the recruitment phase, the pre-ChalleNGe (acclimation) phase, and the ChalleNGe (residential) phase. Outputs are related to cadet activities, including the process of graduating cadets. Outcomes expected to result from the program are divided roughly by time, with the earliest outcomes expected within about three years and the latest ones expected to require at least seven postgraduation years. We refer back to this model in the following chapters when discussing Job ChalleNGe implementation and program outcomes for both Youth and Job ChalleNGe.

---

[11] The annual reports completed as part of this project include Wenger et al., 2021; Wenger, Constant, et al., 2022; and Wenger, Cottrell, and Wrabel, 2023; all annual reports are available at www.rand.org/nsrd/projects/national-guard-challenge.html.

FIGURE 1.1
Youth ChalleNGe Logic Model

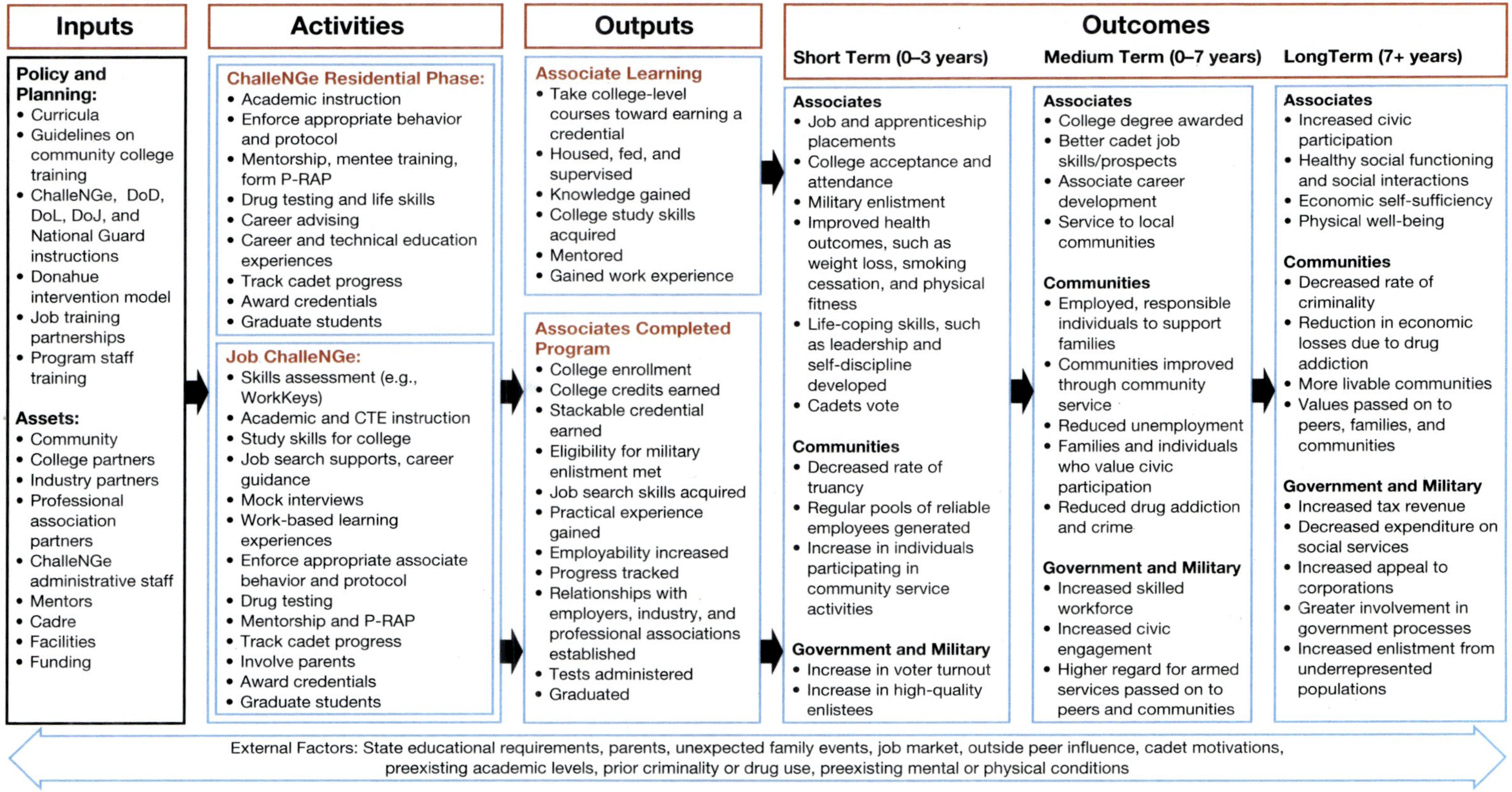

Inputs	Activities	Outputs	Outcomes			
			Short Term (0–3 years)	Medium Term (0–7 years)	LongTerm (7+ years)	

Inputs

Policy and Planning:
- Curricula
- Guidelines on community college training
- ChalleNGe, DoD, DoL, DoJ, and National Guard instructions
- Donahue intervention model
- Job training partnerships
- Program staff training

Assets:
- Community
- College partners
- Industry partners
- Professional association partners
- ChalleNGe administrative staff
- Mentors
- Cadre
- Facilities
- Funding

Activities

ChalleNGe Residential Phase:
- Academic instruction
- Enforce appropriate behavior and protocol
- Mentorship, mentee training, form P-RAP
- Drug testing and life skills
- Career advising
- Career and technical education experiences
- Track cadet progress
- Award credentials
- Graduate students

Job ChalleNGe:
- Skills assessment (e.g., WorkKeys)
- Academic and CTE instruction
- Study skills for college
- Job search supports, career guidance
- Mock interviews
- Work-based learning experiences
- Enforce appropriate associate behavior and protocol
- Drug testing
- Mentorship and P-RAP
- Track cadet progress
- Involve parents
- Award credentials
- Graduate students

Outputs

Associate Learning
- Take college-level courses toward earning a credential
- Housed, fed, and supervised
- Knowledge gained
- College study skills acquired
- Mentored
- Gained work experience

Associates Completed Program
- College enrollment
- College credits earned
- Stackable credential earned
- Eligibility for military enlistment met
- Job search skills acquired
- Practical experience gained
- Employability increased
- Progress tracked
- Relationships with employers, industry, and professional associations established
- Tests administered
- Graduated

Outcomes

Short Term (0–3 years)

Associates
- Job and apprenticeship placements
- College acceptance and attendance
- Military enlistment
- Improved health outcomes, such as weight loss, smoking cessation, and physical fitness
- Life-coping skills, such as leadership and self-discipline developed
- Cadets vote

Communities
- Decreased rate of truancy
- Regular pools of reliable employees generated
- Increase in individuals participating in community service activities

Government and Military
- Increase in voter turnout
- Increase in high-quality enlistees

Medium Term (0–7 years)

Associates
- College degree awarded
- Better cadet job skills/prospects
- Associate career development
- Service to local communities

Communities
- Employed, responsible individuals to support families
- Communities improved through community service
- Reduced unemployment
- Families and individuals who value civic participation
- Reduced drug addiction and crime

Government and Military
- Increased skilled workforce
- Increased civic engagement
- Higher regard for armed services passed on to peers and communities

LongTerm (7+ years)

Associates
- Increased civic participation
- Healthy social functioning and social interactions
- Economic self-sufficiency
- Physical well-being

Communities
- Decreased rate of criminality
- Reduction in economic losses due to drug addiction
- More livable communities
- Values passed on to peers, families, and communities

Government and Military
- Increased tax revenue
- Decreased expenditure on social services
- Increased appeal to corporations
- Greater involvement in government processes
- Increased enlistment from underrepresented populations

External Factors: State educational requirements, parents, unexpected family events, job market, outside peer influence, cadet motivations, preexisting academic levels, prior criminality or drug use, preexisting mental or physical conditions

SOURCE: Features information collected from the National Guard Youth ChalleNGe sites (see Wenger et al., 2017) and refinements based on feedback collected from stakeholders since 2017. DoJ = Department of Justice; DoL = Department of Labor.

Contribution and Organization of This Report

The analyses we present in this capstone report build on and extend prior research that RAND researchers have conducted on ChalleNGe. That research has been presented in the annual reports discussed previously; RAND's capstone report from the first ChalleNGe study, which launched in fiscal year 2017 (see Wenger, Wrabel, et al., 2022); and the pilot studies previously mentioned. This report extends those analyses by examining ChalleNGe's alignment with its mission to serve at-risk youth to identify trends in participation using data beyond those provided by ChalleNGe sites, identify available approaches to measure longer-term outcomes and assess those approaches, and help program leadership at DoD, the National Guard Bureau, and the sites gain a deeper understanding of program implementation and outcomes.

Chapter 2 includes a description of the Youth and Job ChalleNGe participants; we also compare the participants with other young people in the United States and briefly discuss relevant trends in secondary education and juvenile justice. Chapter 3 documents the Job ChalleNGe implementation study; Chapter 4 documents the Job ChalleNGe outcomes study. Chapter 5 details the key findings of this research and our recommendations and future directions for ChalleNGe research.

CHAPTER 2

Youth ChalleNGe Participants and Their Home Communities

Completing high school and entering the labor force are key steps in young people's development; success in these areas is a strong predictor of long-term success (Mortimer, 2003). But each year in the United States, hundreds of thousands of young people leave high school without a diploma, and many others who remain in school do not earn credits at a pace necessary to graduate on time. While some members of this group move successfully into the labor force, many young people who lack a diploma or training struggle. As of this writing, the unemployment rate among 16- to 19-year-olds without a high school diploma is 15.3 percent, which is substantially higher than the total U.S. rate of 3.9 percent but lower than the average youth unemployment rate of roughly 20 percent when we consider the period since 2000 (U.S. Bureau of Labor Statistics, undated).

The Youth and Job ChalleNGe programs were developed to serve young people who have left high school without a credential and those who are not on track to graduate and who need additional training to succeed in the labor force.[1] Implicit in this objective is an effort to target resources to young people experiencing significant levels of economic hardship. In this chapter, we provide information about current trends that influence the number of young people who may seek to enter Youth ChalleNGe and the types of services they are likely to require. Additionally, we describe the communities where cadets lived prior to entering Youth ChalleNGe, with a focus on trends over time and variation in communities.

Trends in the U.S. Youth Population

To better understand the number of young people who make up the potential pool of Youth ChalleNGe participants, we describe the overall level of educational attainment in the United States, as well as rates of arrest and use of mental health services. The logic behind considering these specific trends is based on Youth ChalleNGe's mission to serve those without a high

---

[1] Recall that the Youth ChalleNGe program was designed for students who had left high school without a credential and those at risk of dropping out. This distinction is influenced by state policy; states differ in the age and circumstances at which they allow students to leave high school.

school credential and the fact that an arrest or a mental health diagnosis may disqualify a young person from entering Youth ChalleNGe.

The total population of young people (defined as those aged 16–24) has remained relatively stable over the past two decades, while the proportion who graduate from high school has increased substantially; indeed, the number of students who leave high school without a credential (traditionally referred to as *dropouts*) has fallen by about 50 percent over the past 20 years (de Brey, Zhang, and Duffy, 2022, Table 219.20).[2] This is good news, especially given the evidence that at least some of this increase reflects greater learning due to federally driven school accountability policy.[3] Although the Youth ChalleNGe program currently has the capacity to serve only a fraction of those who leave high school without a diploma, the size and speed of this change suggest that the pool of potential Youth ChalleNGe applicants is smaller today than in the past, and those who leave school without a credential today may have different characteristics than in the past. Specifically, students who leave school without a credential today may be less prepared academically or may require more services and supports than was the case in the past.[4] Additionally, a variety of alternative schools and programs proliferated during this time that directly compete with the credit recovery and credential completion aspects of Youth ChalleNGe.[5] All of these suggest that the pool of potential cadets is smaller today and that these young people may be less prepared than the average cadet in the past.

Over the past two decades, rates of arrest among adolescents have decreased dramatically. The trend holds across types of arrest—those for property crimes, drug-related crimes, and violent crimes; however, the source or sources of this change are not well understood (National Center for Juvenile Justice, 2022). This trend is likely to increase the potential pool of Youth ChalleNGe participants and could change the pool in other ways, too. Finally, reported levels of major depression and reported use of mental health services both increased during the pandemic; this appears to be a continuation of a trend that started around 2010 (Substance Abuse and Mental Health Services Administration, 2022). This suggests that future cadets could require higher levels of support and services than was the case in the past. Tracking these and similar trends will be important for Youth ChalleNGe as the programs

---

[2] See Stetser and Stillwell, 2014, for more information on how the number of high school graduates is calculated.

[3] See, among others, Harris et al., 2020; these authors find that the increase in high school graduation rates was linked to the passage of the No Child Left Behind legislation in 2001 (Pub. L. 107-110, 2002). Aside from these longer trends, the COVID-19 pandemic caused severe short-term disruptions; see, among others, Booher-Jennings, 2005; Kreig, 2008; Neal and Schanzenbach, 2010.

[4] See, among others, Booher-Jennings, 2005; Kreig, 2008; Neal and Schanzenbach, 2010.

[5] In 2001, 39 percent of public-school districts reported offering at least one alternative school; by 2008, 64 percent of school district superintendents reported having alternative schools or programs available in their district (Carver, Lewis, and Tice, 2010; Kleiner, Porch, and Farris, 2002). We note that these two figures are drawn from different sources and that the 2008 survey include schools and programs. More-precise information is not available because there is no national database of alternative programs. Our interpretation of these figures is that alternative programs became more widely available during this period.

continue to serve young people. Along with an understanding of relevant trends, the programs could benefit from additional information on the backgrounds of cadets. Therefore, in the next section of this chapter, we compare the home communities that Youth ChalleNGe cadets come from with all other communities in the United States; we make these comparisons on a wide variety of measures related to economic hardship and well-being. Put differently, our research question for this section of the chapter is, "To what extent does the Youth ChalleNGe program serve young people from disadvantaged communities?" We also present some analyses comparing the communities of various subgroups of cadets. Within this section, we also describe the data used in our analysis, as well as the limitations of this descriptive work. We close with a short summary of our key findings.

Describing Youth ChalleNGe Cadets' Communities

To the extent that the Youth ChalleNGe program helps cadets from disadvantaged communities finish high school and connect with opportunities for further education, training, or jobs, this suggests that the program is well positioned to achieve its mission. Additionally, gaining a deeper understanding of cadets' backgrounds and communities may provide insights for program staff as they consider how best to recruit and serve participants.

The data collected by the RAND team on Youth ChalleNGe cadets from 2016 to 2021 reveal that the average Youth ChalleNGe cadet is a 16-year-old male with academic achievement below grade-level by several academic years.[6] (The program does serve female cadets, but the majority of cadets are male.) The majority of cadets identify as Black, Latino, Asian or Pacific Islander, or Native American/American Indian, although this varies by site and state. The ChalleNGe program is not means-tested, meaning that participants may be admitted regardless of their family income, and little information is collected about cadets' communities or family resources. Our previous reports have focused on program- and cadet-level measures of success and differences in policies or practices across sites rather than on cadets' backgrounds.[7] In this section, we combine data from multiple sources to learn more about cadets' backgrounds and home communities.

Data and Methods

The data used to examine Youth ChalleNGe cadets' communities came from three different sources.[8] Data on the Youth ChalleNGe cadets, covering those who entered the program

---

[6] Youth ChalleNGe uses a standardized test, the Test of Adult Basic Education, to assess cadets' initial achievement and their academic performance at the end of the program.

[7] All reports completed as part of RAND's work with ChalleNGe are available at www.rand.org/nsrd/projects/national-guard-challenge.html.

[8] Our analyses include information on all young people who enter pre-ChalleNGe. The vast majority of these Youth ChalleNGe participants complete the initial two-week pre-ChalleNGe program and enter

between 2016 and 2021, were extracted from the data provided annually by Youth ChalleNGe sites to RAND.[9] These data do not contain any personal identifiers, but they do include indicators of each cadet's race and ethnicity, gender, home zip code, age, program site, and class. These individual-level data were merged with zip code–level measures of social capital and economic connections gathered by Opportunity Insights, as well as demographic measures of income, poverty, labor force participation, family structure, and other similar information from the American Community Survey (ACS).[10] The measures of social capital and economic connectedness calculate the share of high socioeconomic status (SES) friends among individuals with low SES. The data also include measures of clustering to determine how many of an individual's friends are also friends with each other, as well as membership in online groups devoted to volunteering or other civic organizations.[11] Measures from the ACS include community-level data on race and ethnicity, education levels, median income, poverty rates, and labor force participation. While we use the word *community* to describe the level of our analyses, the data are organized by zip code.[12]

After we merged data from these three sources, our analytic dataset contained information on about 64,300 cadets.[13] We generated descriptive statistics for each measure of social

---

Youth ChalleNGe; at that point, the participants are formally referred to as *cadets*. For simplicity here, we refer to the participants in our analyses as *cadets*.

[9] The RAND team has received consistent, individual-level data on Youth ChalleNGe cadets from 2015 to 2021; the team has not received similar data on the newer and smaller Job ChalleNGe program. Therefore, our analyses reported here focus on Youth ChalleNGe. The findings may be relevant to Job ChalleNGe, whose participants are Youth ChalleNGe graduates. Additionally, we explore and discuss some of the differences between Youth ChalleNGe and Job ChalleNGe participants in a single state in Chapter 4. Finally, though we have data on Youth ChalleNGe cadets from 2015, we do not have their zip codes, and so this year of data is excluded from our analyses.

[10] *High* and *low* SES are defined in terms of median income; individuals in households with incomes greater than the county-level median are considered to be of high SES, and those in households with incomes less than the county-level median are considered to be of low SES. See Opportunity Insights (undated) and Appendix A for more information about these data.

[11] For more information on the social capital data, which are based on data collected from Facebook users, see Opportunity Insights (undated). For a detailed description of these data, see Chetty et al., 2022. Note that the Opportunity Insights data are not panel data; rather, they are available at a single point in time, typically 2018. The ACS variables come from the five-year 2016–2020 sample (U.S. Census Bureau, 2022). Appendix A also includes more information about the variables derived from these data sources and the sample.

[12] To be more precise, our data are measured at the zip code level. Using zip codes has advantages over using more-aggregated measures, such as Metropolitan Statistical Areas or counties. There are more than 41,000 zip codes in the United States (U.S. Postal Service, undated) versus about 3,000 counties. Some zip codes, such as the one assigned to the Pentagon, are not linked to residential areas; these zip codes with no residents are excluded from our analyses. Our choice to use zip codes was also driven by data availability; for example, we have zip codes for cadets' home residences, but we do not have street addresses or more-precise measures of geography.

[13] For more details on the dataset, see Appendix A.

capital and of economic hardship, and then we compared the means and standard errors on these measures for Youth ChalleNGe cadets with the population-weighted means for all zip codes.[14] We then carried out subgroup analyses comparing the average community of cadets by race and ethnicity and gender over time. Finally, we tested the data for notable time trends to see whether there was a shift in the type of communities that cadets came from over the time covered by our data—given the disruptions posed by the pandemic, we were interested to learn how the communities of cadets who entered Youth ChalleNGe during the pandemic compared with the communities of cadets who entered the program prior to the pandemic.[15] We present these results in turn.

Comparing Cadets' Neighborhoods with All U.S. Neighborhoods

Figure 2.1 includes measures of poverty, education, labor force participation, and social capital; in each case, we calculate the average for cadets' communities and for all U.S. communities.[16] ChalleNGe cadets' communities are more disadvantaged than the average U.S. community on every dimension examined.[17] Cadets' communities are poorer (in terms of household and child poverty rates) than the average U.S. community. Cadets' communities have, on average, lower levels of education and youth labor force participation than other communities. The average median income in Youth ChalleNGe cadet zip codes is approximately $10,000 less than the U.S. average and non–Youth ChalleNGe zip codes. Cadets' communities also score lower on economic connectedness; this is the measure of online connections between low-socioeconomic-status and high-socioeconomic-status individuals within a zip code.[18] There are statistically significant, but smaller, differences in volunteering rates and civic organizations observed as well. All of these measures have been shown to be positively connected to the level of economic mobility in an area (Chetty et al., 2022). Taken

---

[14] We also looked at differences between zip codes that had sent any Youth ChalleNGe participants and those that had not, also weighted by population. Only about one-third of zip codes in either dataset had sent at least one cadet in any of the six years in our sample, indicating substantial concentration in the areas that cadets come from. These results are found in Appendix A and generally match the analysis comparing cadets' communities with all zip codes.

[15] We tested the significance of the overall differences and differences between subgroups using two-way t-tests; we supplemented these tests with regression analyses. We used ordinary least squares (OLS) regression models comparing the race, gender, and year variables with each outcome variable of interest. We also tested models that further controlled for census divisions; finally, we tested for within versus between site-level effects using fixed-effects models. Our regressions analyses (excluded for brevity) confirmed the results observed in descriptive analyses.

[16] We weighted the results by the number of observations in each case (by the number of cadets and by the population, respectively).

[17] We examined other measures from the ACS (for example, overall unemployment rate); the results were comparable to those shown in Figure 2.1.

[18] The average Youth ChalleNGe cadet comes from a community with a level of economic connectedness of 39 percent, compared with the U.S. average of 43 percent.

together, these results are not surprising; indeed, the patterns suggest that the program is meeting an aspect of its mission to serve students who face considerable disadvantages.

FIGURE 2.1

Differences in Youth ChalleNGe Cadets' Neighborhoods and U.S. Average Levels of Economic Hardship

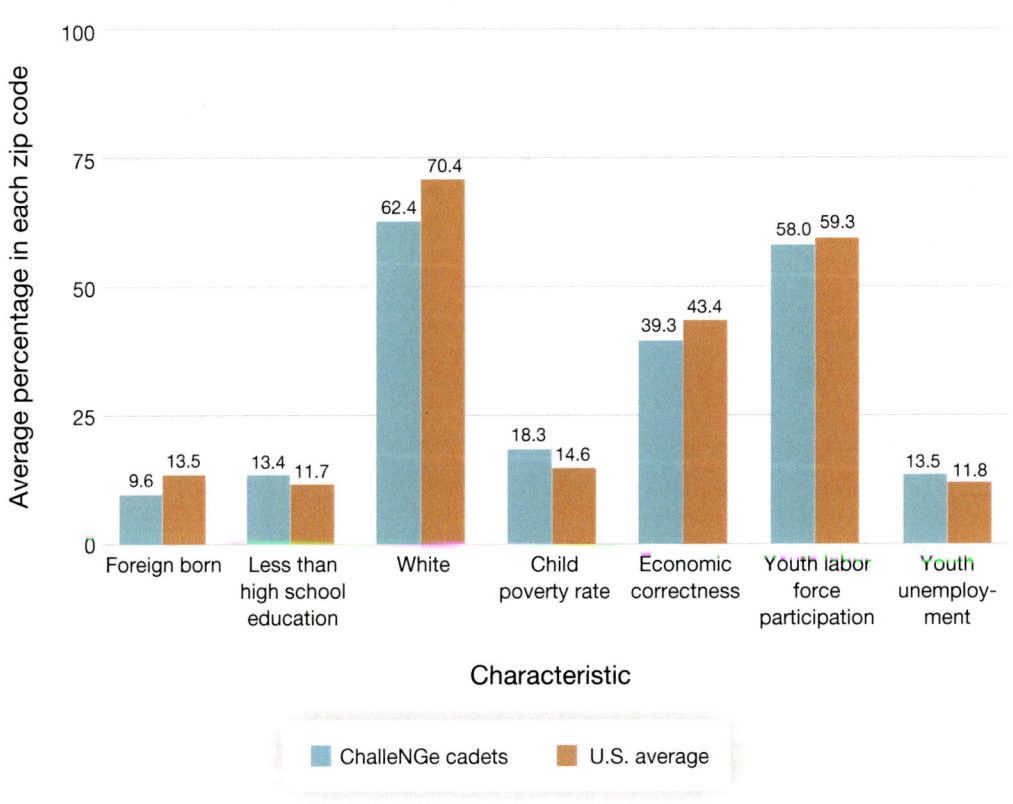

SOURCES: Authors' calculations from RAND annual collections, Youth ChalleNGe classes including 2016–2021; ACS five-year averages, 2016–2020 (U.S. Census Bureau, 2022); and Opportunity Insights data (Opportunity Insights, undated). These sources are described in more detail at the beginning of this chapter and in Appendix A.

Subgroup Analysis: Comparing the Neighborhoods of Different Groups of Cadets

Next, we compare the communities of cadets of different racial and ethnic backgrounds.[19] Among ChalleNGe cadets, there are substantial differences in the measures presented in Figure 2.1 by race and ethnicity. The communities that non-White cadets come from are significantly different and less economically advantaged than the backgrounds of White cadets on virtually every dimension. White cadets, relative to non-White cadets, come from communities with higher proportions of White residents and with a lower percentage of foreign-born residents. Non-White cadets come from communities that generally have higher proportions of non-White residents but also lower levels of education and youth labor force participation. Child poverty and youth unemployment rates are also both higher for non-White cadets' communities than for the communities from which White cadets come. Finally, economic connectedness is lower in non-White cadets' communities, indicating that these cadets generally come from communities where economic mobility could be expected to be lower.

A comparison of Figure 2.1 with Figure 2.2 suggests that the differences in cadets' communities versus the average U.S. community are driven by the characteristics of non-White cadets' communities. This likely reflects two factors: First, the majority of Youth ChalleNGe cadets are non-White; and second, there is considerable residential segregation in the United States, both by income and by race and ethnicity.[20]

Have Cadets' Neighborhoods Varied over Time?

The number of Youth ChalleNGe cadets fell sharply during the pandemic (Wenger, Cottrell, and Wrabel, 2023); the sites may have attracted and admitted participants from different backgrounds during this period. To test this, we look at the economic and social measures described previously on a yearly basis.[21] But when we look at these measures for all cadets by year, there is evidence that from 2020 onward, cadets came from somewhat less disadvantaged communities than in prior years (2016–2019). The differences show up in household and child poverty rates and also in youth labor force participation, youth unemployment, and social connectedness. Poverty and unemployment rates declined somewhat over time, while social connectedness and youth labor force participation increased somewhat. The magnitudes of these shifts are relatively small when compared with the overall differences described earlier but still amount to about a 1-percent decrease in poverty rates over the time

---

[19] We have a sufficient sample size to compare cadets who identify as *White* with those who identify as part of another group; we refer to the latter group as *non-White*.

[20] See, among others, Taylor and Fry, 2012, and Boustan, 2013. Boustan, 2013, also documents the negative effect of residential segregation on economic outcomes.

[21] Note that the measures for a given neighborhood do not change over time; the social connectedness data were measured at a point in time, and the economic measures from the ACS were based on five years of data.

FIGURE 2.2

Differences in Youth ChalleNGe Cadets' Neighborhoods, by Race and Ethnicity

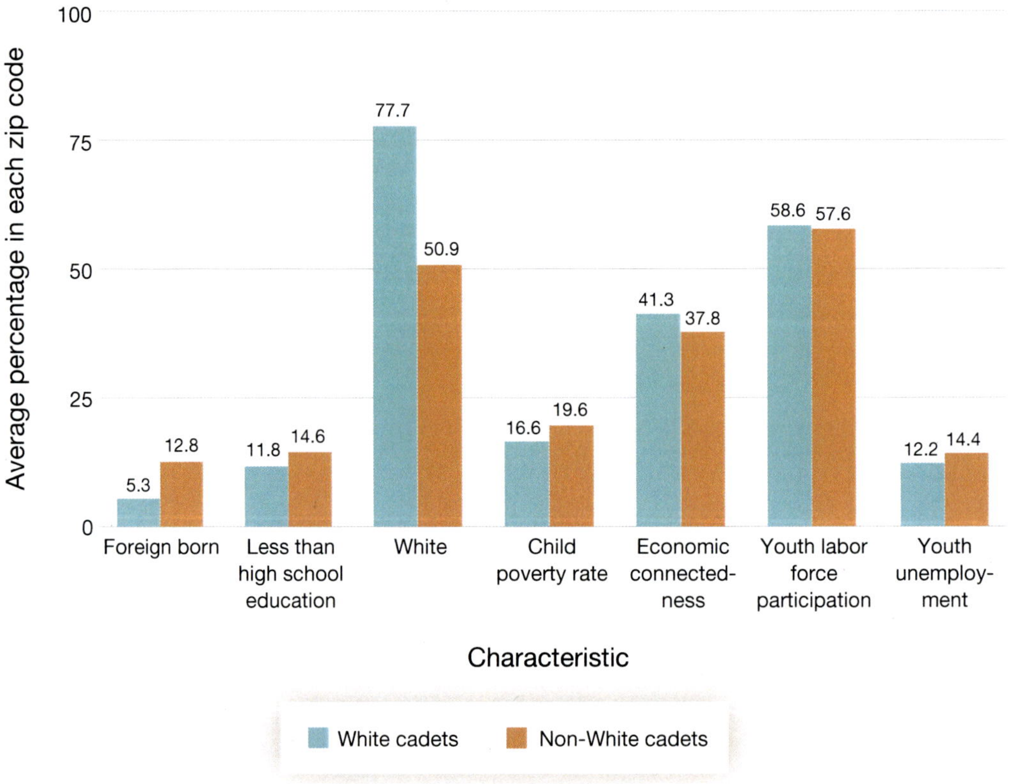

SOURCES: Authors' calculations from RAND annual collections, Youth ChalleNGe classes including 2016–2021; American Community Survey five-year averages, 2016–2020 (U.S. Census Bureau, 2022); and Opportunity Insights data (Opportunity Insights, undated). These sources are described in more detail at the beginning of this chapter and in Appendix A.

frame covered; the differences remain after controlling for race and ethnicity, gender, and the Youth ChalleNGe site's region as defined by census divisions.[22]

This average shift could indicate that recruiting cadets from the most disadvantaged communities became more difficult in recent years, an increase in demand for Youth ChalleNGe from somewhat more advantaged communities, or both. These results suggest that the types

---

[22] To better understand the relationships between these measures, we used OLS regression models. This technique allowed us to look at the difference in each outcome variable while holding other factors constant. We find that the time trends described here remain when we hold constant cadet characteristics (race and ethnicity and gender), when we correct for site-level differences, and when we correct for differences at the census division level. This indicates that the differences over time are not driven by recruiting cadets with different characteristics or by changes in recruiting across sites or regions, but that, within sites, the type of neighborhoods that cadets have come from has shifted during recent years to slightly less disadvantaged communities.

of communities that cadets have come from have slowly shifted over time to slightly less disadvantaged communities. This trend is more notable among non-White cadets. While household and child poverty rates and youth unemployment decreased for both groups over time, the decline was greater among non-White cadets. These group differences were not substantial enough to remove the differences in community background highlighted previously but did close the gap on some of these measures.

We may see this trend reverse as the programs continue to recover from the pandemic. Regardless, this trend suggests that sites should assess how their recruiting may have explicitly or implicitly changed during and after the pandemic and the extent to which they continue to serve the least advantaged areas in their states.

Limitations

The analysis conducted here is purely descriptive, highlighting differences between communities (defined by zip codes) that Youth ChalleNGe cadets come from versus national averages or measures in communities that did not send any cadets to the Youth ChalleNGe program. While regression analyses were conducted to compare the statistical significance of observed differences by demographic variables and over time, we cannot draw causal claims about the direction of these relationships or what specific attributes may have caused any shifts over time.

Additionally, merged data from both the Opportunity Insights and ACS datasets represent community (zip code–level) averages rather than measures at the individual level. Thus, the comparisons made here are between the average person in one zip code and the average person in another zip code. Doing so allows us to make comparisons about what these cadets' communities look like, but *not* about what their specific households look like. Additionally, the Opportunity Insights data are derived from data on Facebook connections between individuals of different socioeconomic backgrounds. Some individuals are not present on Facebook, and presence on the platform may vary across zip codes; this represents another potential limitation to the data. That said, Facebook usage is highly prevalent, and most zip codes with small numbers of individuals are excluded from the Opportunity Insights data files (for more information, see Opportunity Insights, undated).

Finally, neither the Opportunity Insights nor the ACS data include information on every single population zip code in the United States. The main omission from both datasets is Puerto Rico. As a result, all ChalleNGe cadets who attend the program in Puerto Rico are excluded from the analysis. Additionally, both data providers mask smaller zip codes where the number of respondents is below a certain threshold. While most Youth ChalleNGe cadets were matched to a zip code in both the Opportunity Insights and ACS data, a small proportion of cadets came from zip codes that were excluded from one or both datasets (see Appendix A for more information on the sample).

Conclusion

In this chapter, we document substantial evidence that the Youth ChalleNGe program serves young people from poorly resourced neighborhoods. Cadets' neighborhoods are less advantaged than other neighborhoods in terms of annual earnings, labor force participation, poverty, and social connectedness. This indicates that the program is serving its target population and meeting its mission. The differences in social connectedness may be especially salient for cadets because they often move back to their home neighborhoods to search for work.

Among cadets, we find that non-White cadets come from neighborhoods that are considerably more disadvantaged than those of White cadets. These differences, which extend to the measures of social connectedness, are reflective of the overall patterns of racial and ethnic (as well as economic) segregation in the United States. This result suggests that some cadets may require additional supports as they return to their poorly resourced neighborhoods.

Since the pandemic began, the population of cadets has changed slightly—cadets, and especially non-White cadets, come from slightly less disadvantaged neighborhoods than was the case prior to the pandemic. The drivers of this trend are not clear, and it may reverse in the future. Program sites may wish to examine their recruiting practices or geographic data on their current classes to better understand this trend.

Finally, we document several relevant trends external to Youth ChalleNGe. The number of people leaving high school without a credential has fallen sharply over the past two decades, but there is evidence that those who leave school without a diploma (and enter Youth ChalleNGe) today may require more services than cadets in the past. Other trends will have mixed or uncertain effects on Youth ChalleNGe. Reported levels of major depression and use of mental health services have increased during the pandemic, a continuation of a longer trend. This suggests that an increasing proportion of cadets may require additional supports and that sites may wish to screen applicants carefully to ensure that the program can provide appropriate supports. Rates of arrest among adolescents have fallen dramatically—this trend also began prior to the pandemic. This could result in a larger pool of potential cadets, but again, these candidates may require additional assistance (the reason or reasons behind the decrease in adolescent arrests are not yet well understood). Taken as a group, these trends suggest that while adolescents who struggle in traditional schools may differ from past cohorts in some ways and may require additional support, there remain many young people who could benefit from taking part in Youth ChalleNGe.

CHAPTER 3

Job ChalleNGe Implementation

The Job ChalleNGe program, available only to graduates of Youth ChalleNGe, is a five-and-a-half-month residential program that builds on the academic and career development foundations of Youth ChalleNGe. Participants in Job ChalleNGe have the opportunity to complete their high school diploma or equivalency, if they have not yet done so, as well as pursue postsecondary training in one of a number of career fields (varying by site). We provide a detailed summary of the Job ChalleNGe program in Chapter 1 of this report. At the time of our data collection activities, Job ChalleNGe was offered in six states: California, Georgia, Louisiana, Michigan, South Carolina, and West Virginia.[1]

The Job ChalleNGe experience may vary within and across sites: Sites offer different residential facilities and structures, training programs, and opportunities for recreation and service. Cadre, staff who work with and monitor participants, have different professional backgrounds and approaches by site. Within a single site and class, participants take different courses that meet on different schedules and vary in terms of their duration (i.e., from two months to the maximum five-and-a-half months). Sites have different policies related to opportunities for participants to visit home; home visits are offered with different frequency, duration, and guidance on a site-by-site basis. Sites also place a differential emphasis on the eight core components that guide the Youth ChalleNGe program. Some emphasize all eight core components, while others focus on specific facets of development, and all have a particular emphasis on job skills.

In this chapter, we describe findings from the analysis of two data collection efforts. First, we issued a standardized information request of Job ChalleNGe sites in summer 2022, in which staff for each site provided information related to overall program operations. Second, the research team conducted Job ChalleNGe site visits in spring 2023 to collect insights and perspectives from staff and participants.[2] The overarching question we answer in this chapter is "How does Job ChalleNGe prepare participants for program and postprogram success?"

---

[1] In July 2023, Louisiana Job ChalleNGe started a new operating agreement with the National Guard Bureau (previously, this site operated with Department of Labor funding). DoD now funds eight Job ChalleNGe sites, although New Mexico's and Oklahoma's programs are in the development stage and will not serve participants until 2025 at the earliest.

[2] Participants in the Job ChalleNGe program have different titles at different programs. For simplicity, we refer to them all as *participants* here.

Prior Job ChalleNGe Findings and Study Contribution

Our data collection and analysis efforts were designed to build on our prior findings regarding Job ChalleNGe program implementation. In our prior research on Job ChalleNGe (Wenger, Constant, et al., 2022), we described the implementation of the Job ChalleNGe program across the six sites, leveraging analysis from interviews that we conducted virtually with site leadership and staff in 2021. We focused our implementation analysis on the goals and core components of the program; the ways that program features, policies, and processes align with program design; each site's partnerships with community colleges and adult learning centers; and barriers and facilitators to implementation.

We found that the sites demonstrated many strengths, yet they faced challenges typical of initial program startup and ongoing maintenance. Chief among the sites' strengths was that program staff demonstrated strong buy-in for the Job ChalleNGe missions. Staff buy-in was key to the successes that sites were achieving, and staff were confident in their ability to strengthen the program due to their investment and collaboration. Site staff described their successes and challenges developing and maintaining key partnerships that are central to the Job ChalleNGe program and the participants' experiences: partnerships with education institutions and training organizations to provide participants with appropriate and sufficient academic and career development, as well as partnerships with local and regional employers to facilitate participants' hiring into training-aligned jobs after program graduation. Some challenges with ongoing and potential partnerships were rooted in schedule and calendar misalignment between Job ChalleNGe and partners, the logistics of transporting participants to their classes, and participants' preparation for coursework and job placement.

Our prior analyses allowed us to illuminate details regarding program structure and offerings and staff and leadership perspectives on implementation. One gap in our research is that we had yet to include the critical perspectives of participants and their firsthand accounts of the program experience. This report fills that gap for Job ChalleNGe and includes participant perspectives regarding the Job ChalleNGe experience and the available services and resources to support their success in the program and beyond.

Data and Methods

We gathered data through two sources: (1) a standardized information request in summer 2022 and (2) site visits in spring 2023 to the six operating Job ChalleNGe sites, where we conducted interviews with staff and focus groups with participants.

Standardized Information Request

We sent an information request in the form of a spreadsheet to each Job ChalleNGe site director. The request included 24 questions that focused on training programs, services, personnel, and funding. Examples of questions include the following:

- Have you added any training programs for the 2022 classes? Please list.
- For the spring 2021 and fall 2021 classes, what facilities or services did Job ChalleNGe provide participants?
- Are there any barriers to providing other services that participants need?
- Please provide the number of staff in each position (e.g., cadre).
- Do you partner with local and regional employers to place graduates in their field of study?
- For the spring 2021 and fall 2021 classes, please account for all sources of funding by filling in the boxes.

For the purpose of this chapter, we identified relevant data points from the standardized information request and integrated them into our qualitative findings. Data from the standardized information request are referenced in our findings when we describe what a site or sites reported (e.g., "All sites reported").

Staff Interviews and Participant Focus Groups

We visited each Job ChalleNGe site between February and April 2023 over the course of one to two days, depending on participant schedules and site priorities. During these site visits, we conducted fact-finding interviews with select staff to build on our prior interviews. We also had the opportunity to conduct focus groups with site participants.[3]

For the staff interviews, we recruited key staff members who could best offer insights on the services and resources provided to help participants meet Job ChalleNGe expectations. Broadly, this meant connecting with staff who had a direct role in promoting academic excellence, fostering physical and mental wellness, and preparing participants for post–Job ChalleNGe opportunities (see Table 3.1 for the number of interviews and focus groups conducted at each site). One-on-one interviews with staff ranged from 40 to 60 minutes.

For the focus groups, we worked with site staff to identify participants who were age-eligible to participate (i.e., at least 18 years of age). From the pool of eligible participants, we asked sites to form two focus groups with no more than 10 participants in a single group. We worked with Job ChalleNGe sites to recruit individuals who were enrolled across all training tracks and represented the diversity of participant backgrounds. However, availability to participate was constrained by participants' schedules and ages. Two sites each formed a single focus group because of either a limited pool of eligible participants or challenges

---

[3] Clearance for these focus groups was provided by the Office of Management and Budget (Control Number: 0704-0642).

TABLE 3.1

Number of Interviews and Focus Groups, by Site

Job ChalleNGe Site	Staff Interviews	Participant Focus Groups	Focus Group Participants
California	3	2	11
Georgia	4	2	7
Louisiana	3	1	9
Michigan	3	1	7
South Carolina	4	2	7
West Virginia	3	2	12

related to participants' schedules and availabilities. Participants in the focus groups across these two sites represented a mix of trade programs. At sites that were able to form two focus groups, we asked that one of the two groups represent a single training track so that we could better explore the shared academic experiences of participants. In total, our focus groups engaged with 53 participants representing most but not all training tracks offered by the Job ChalleNGe sites. Focus groups with participants lasted 75–90 minutes.

Focus group participants completed an anonymous demographic background sheet that included five questions: age, educational attainment prior to Job ChalleNGe, parent's or guardian's educational level, job training track, and post–Job ChalleNGe plans. We provide aggregate responses to these questions in Tables 3.2 and 3.3. The data collected through this background sheet were not linked to participants' responses in the focus group. The key takeaway from these demographic characteristics is that our sample includes a wide variety of individuals. The modal participant was 18 years of age (68 percent) and arrived at Job ChalleNGe having already earned a high school diploma or equivalent (74 percent). Most participants also reported having at least one parent with a high school degree (including a high school equivalency degree) or more (66 percent). Participants were enrolled in 14 different training tracks, with construction and welding (32 percent) and heavy equipment operator (19 percent) being the most common. Notably, 4 percent of the participants were studying for their high school diploma equivalency degree rather than pursuing a job training track. In regard to participants' plans after completion of Job ChalleNGe, participants were given 13 options and were asked to select all that applied. More than half of the participants planned to secure a new job (55 percent), although only 7 percent identified this as their only post–Job ChalleNGe plan. Many participants also indicated intent to join the armed services (45 percent), and for one-fourth of these participants, this was their only post–Job ChalleNGe plan. Lastly, a little more than half of participants planned to obtain a license or certificate in a career field (51 percent), but they were also planning to pursue at least one additional option.

We used Dedoose, a qualitative analytic software, for our deductive analysis of interviews and focus groups. We developed a codebook that was derived from our logic model, research question, and prior data collection (see Wenger, Constant, et al., 2022) for this project to ensure that we captured evidence to answer the main research question. Our coding scheme captured the background of participants, program structure, educational programming, supports and services, program resources, and opportunities and challenges. Once codes were applied to the data, we reviewed codes and the interactions between codes to develop themes for the key topics in this section—this process also included several discussions for researchers to deliberate on and reconcile conflicting analyses. In our presentation of findings, we identify the data that came from interviews and focus groups.

TABLE 3.2

Demographic Characteristics of Job ChalleNGe Focus Group Participants, Aggregated Across Sites

Demographic Characteristics	Proportion of Focus Group Participants
Age	
18	68
19	19
20+	4
Unknown	9
Educational attainment prior to Job ChalleNGe	
High school diploma or equivalent	74
Working toward a high school diploma	17
No high school diploma or equivalent	2
Unclear or unreported	8
Parent or guardian education level	
Some high school	8
Completed high school	25
Completed a GED, HiSET, or equivalent	11
Some college beyond high school (including trade schools)	11
Completed college or trade school	15
Graduate or professional school	4
Other, do not know, not applicable, or unclear	26

NOTE: Numbers may total to more than 100 percent due to rounding; demographic characteristics of all participants across the six sites are not available. HiSET = High School Equivalency Test.

TABLE 3.3

Job ChalleNGe Training Program and Post-Program Plans Among Focus Group Participants, Aggregated Across Sites

Characteristics	Proportion of Focus Group Participants
Job ChalleNGe training track	
Information technology	9
Automotive	8
Health professions	15
Construction and welding	32
Culinary arts	2
Heavy equipment operator	19
HiSET	4
HVAC	6
Unclear	6
Post–Job ChalleNGe plans (select all that apply)	
Get a new job	55
Return to a previous job	6
Attend a registered apprenticeship program	11
Join the armed services	45
Obtain a license or certificate in a career field	51
Enroll in an associate's degree program	13
Enroll in a bachelor's degree program	19
Participate in a national service program (e.g., AmeriCorps, YouthBuild)	11
Do volunteer or missionary work	13
Travel	36
Start a family	23
Not sure	13
Other	6

NOTE: *Information technology* also includes administrative technology, robotic programming, and C++. *Health professions* includes certified nursing assistant, medical, patient care, and phlebotomy. HVAC = heating, ventilation, and air conditioning.

Limitations

There are limitations to our findings. First, data from the standardized information request are self-reported. Responses are not free of social bias, and respondents may not have recalled all the details necessary to complete the request. Second, we conducted interviews and focus groups with a sample of site leadership and staff and program participants, respectively, across the six sites. The insights shared through these qualitative data collection activities do not represent the views of all sites, staff, and program participants. We recruited staff for interviews based on their roles, so the staff perspectives are representative of staff by role across sites. All participants aged 18 and older were offered the opportunity to participate in focus groups, but there may have been differential selection into participation, and we did not capture the perspectives of participants younger than 18 years of age. Lastly, we did not collect staff and program participants' racial and ethnic and gender identities; therefore, we are unable to demonstrate how perspectives may vary by those demographic categories.

Program Implementation Findings

In this section, we present findings drawn from our analysis of various data sources in an effort to answer our overarching question: How does Job ChalleNGe prepare participants for program and post-program success? Our analyses focused on participant perspectives on the Job ChalleNGe program and the services and resources that sites provide to support participants' success in the program and beyond. The descriptive summaries we provide are intended to enhance understanding of how sites converge or vary in their operation and implementation of the program. We have grouped our findings into seven overarching themes: joining Job ChalleNGe, the residential experience, the training programs, available services and supports, personal development and interpersonal skills, the role of education partners, and, finally, budgeting priorities and shortfalls.

Joining Job ChalleNGe

In this section, we detail the themes that emerged with regard to participants' motivations for joining Job ChalleNGe, as well as factors that made them hesitant to join, drawing from participant focus group data. We identified motivations that centered on finding a job and continuing the positive experience of Youth ChalleNGe. The common detractors we identified included negative experiences in Youth ChalleNGe, uncertainty about what the Job ChalleNGe program experience would entail, and concerns about program length. We provide additional detail on these themes in the following paragraphs.

Motivated to Find a Job

Participants reported a variety of motivators for joining Job ChalleNGe; the majority centered on finding a job. Across sites, focus group participants noted their interest in training for and trying out a career, becoming qualified for well-paying jobs by developing skills and earning certificates, qualifying for military enlistment, and strengthening their resumes with career-aligned training and continued ChalleNGe participation. According to one participant, "I want to better myself. I want to get as many certifications so I'll never be out of work when I grow up." As participants discussed the training and career development offered by Job ChalleNGe, they often framed it as an opportunity they would not have otherwise had, either due to cost or educational access, and that it was a situation in which they could not "lose," as they perceived that they could only gain from the opportunity provided by Job ChalleNGe.

Interested in Continuing the ChalleNGe Experience

Other motivators for joining Job ChalleNGe were driven by participants' prior experiences as Youth ChalleNGe cadets. Focus group participants described knowing that returning to the structured environment would be good for keeping them "out of trouble" and "accountable" and would also provide needed supports that they might not otherwise have access to at home. Some participants noted that they had lost or "slipped" from the discipline that they developed during Youth ChalleNGe and wanted to develop it again through the Job ChalleNGe experience. Multiple participants noted that they enjoyed their time in Youth ChalleNGe and joined Job ChalleNGe because they figured they would enjoy this program too.

Hesitant Due to Prior ChalleNGe Experience

We asked participants about what made them hesitant to join Job ChalleNGe, and we found that, likewise, their prior Youth ChalleNGe experience informed their areas of concern. Participants expressed concerns about being away from home or their jobs; the unknowns of the Job ChalleNGe environment and experience; and continuing to live under the ChalleNGe quasi-military structure.

Participants across sites discussed their hesitance to join Job ChalleNGe due to the continued structure and anticipation of punishment for infractions. Several participants noted that after Youth ChalleNGe, they felt like disciplined adults, so it has been disheartening to again be in an environment where there is group accountability for individual mistakes. One participant drew the distinction between the ChalleNGe programs in this way: "Youth ChalleNGe is teaching you how to be an adult; Job ChalleNGe is you being an adult." Sometimes participants described chafing against or having dissatisfaction with program structure, given that they view themselves as adults; they did not feel that they were being treated as such under Job ChalleNGe's structure and discipline system.

Unsure About Program Length

Participants shared conflicting perspectives regarding the length of the program. It was noted by different participants as both a benefit and a detractor from the appeal of the program. Some noted that the program was too short for them to earn meaningful credentials, while others noted that the program was too long and they did not need to attend for so long before leaving to seek employment. As a reminder, the residential phase of Job ChalleNGe runs five-and-a-half months.

The Residential Experience

Job ChalleNGe is a residential program in which participants live in facilities with fellow participants for the duration of the program. Each site has unique residential facilities, and there is some variation to the policies and practices that sites establish for the residential program. For instance, there may be a different cadence or frequency of opportunities to return home, and the program's schedule and facilities may shape engagement with peers. To learn more about the resulting experience for participants, we asked both Job ChalleNGe staff and participants about the residential experience. In this section, we draw on both of these data sources to report on emergent themes about the residential program.

Job ChalleNGe staff noted several benefits to the residential nature of the program, while Job ChalleNGe participants mostly commented on the downsides to residential life. Some staff noted that the home lives of participants have a negative influence on participants' behavior and well-being and that being on site at Job ChalleNGe offers participants stability. Staff members commented that it is difficult for participants to "escape" challenging circumstances at home and that the contrast between Youth ChalleNGe and Job ChalleNGe and the home environment can resurface previous negative habits when participants return home. One staff member reflected that a continuous Youth ChalleNGe to Job ChalleNGe experience might be better for participants' well-being and development.[4] A few staff members noted that Youth ChalleNGe participants need more help with their mental and physical health and their academic development than five months of Youth ChalleNGe can give them, and continuing to Job ChalleNGe provides participants with additional support for their development. The benefits of the residential experience that staff perceived stood in contrast to the articulated participant experience.

Participants expressed some difficulties with residential life. While a few participants complained about the quality of food, participants were mostly nervous about living in the residential environment. One dimension of the residential experience that was frequently cited was difficulty being away from home. Many participants shared being homesick. Participants cited that it was a challenge to spend five and a half months away from family, friends, and pets. This homesickness was exacerbated by limited opportunities to visit home. Participants lamented the lack of home visits and the short length of the home visits that they were granted. Relatedly, participants noted that it was difficult to leave jobs that they had secured, especially knowing that they would not make money during Job ChalleNGe; they worried that they might not readily secure a job after Job ChalleNGe graduation.

Some of the difficulties that participants reported with the residential experience seemed to be rooted in misalignment between expectations set prior to joining Job ChalleNGe and their experiences while in the program. These discussions focused on freedoms and privileges and the maturity level of their peers. For instance, some participants reported that

---

[4] There is often a gap between participants' graduation from Youth ChalleNGe and beginning Job ChalleNGe due to differences in class cycles, availability of slots for the next Job ChalleNGe cycle, or other factors.

they were told by ChalleNGe staff prior to enrollment that they would be able to leave every weekend to visit home; this stood in stark contrast to their experience where home visits were infrequent, which was especially difficult for participants who were homesick. Participants also discussed the misalignment of expectations related to access to their phones and shared that they were told that their phones would be available to them when, in fact, access to their phones was limited, and they often had to earn the privilege of using them.[5] Participants who wanted to speak with family on a regular basis or manage personal matters expressed disappointment in this area. For instance, limited access to their phones made it difficult for one participant to manage personal administrative tasks, stating, "Most of my phone time consists of calling like, people or the bank, or someone to get work done. Recently I've been having a problem with getting my stipend from Youth ChalleNGe, and by the time they give us our phones, the bank is closed. That's a problem. I had to do that myself; my family can't do that."[6]

Participants also criticized the maturity of their fellow peers in the program. When they joined Job ChalleNGe, participants assumed that they would be living and learning with peers who shared a similar level of maturity and professionalism; however, this was not always the case, and it frustrated participants who felt that their experience was hampered by their peers' "immature" behavior. Relatedly, the same participants complained about cadre's inconsistent application of penalties when some of their peers violated a site policy. According to one participant, they would like to see cadre "standing by what they said they would kick you out for. The most severe punishment is room restriction, which is ineffective. [Cadre] say there are many things for which you can get kicked out, but they don't do it." The reduction of freedoms and privileges and the differences in perceived maturity among peers made acclimation to the residential experience of Job ChalleNGe difficult for some participants. Participants suggested that having the opportunity to speak with current Job ChalleNGe participants prior to applying or enrolling in the program would likely have tempered these expectations.

Although participants voiced fewer benefits of living on site, they discussed an appreciation for how their basic needs were being met, which was not always the case at home. One participant noted that the relative benefits of a residential program compared with living on one's own or at home included three meals a day, a safe and warm place to sleep, and motivated peers. Another noted that having a set schedule was a real benefit of the residential program. Participants also noted that doing regular exercise reduced their stress and helped them be healthier.

---

[5] With the exception a small pilot program, Youth ChalleNGe participants are not permitted to have or use cell phones during the program. Job ChalleNGe sites typically provide participants with access to cell phones, although the exact procedures and allowances vary by site.

[6] The participant is referencing a stipend provided by Youth ChalleNGe. These stipends are offered at the discretion of the state's National Guard Bureau and are intended to support the graduate's ongoing success during the Youth ChalleNGe post-residential phase. Not all Youth ChalleNGe programs provide the stipend to graduates.

Training Program

We sought to build on our prior evidence that drew on Job ChalleNGe staff perspectives regarding the implementation of the training program. Therefore, we asked participants to reflect on how their training program was preparing them to achieve their professional goals. Several key themes emerged in participants' reflections, including the value of the Job ChalleNGe training program; the instructional style, activities, and supports embedded in their coursework; and perceptions of limitations of the training, in terms of content, nature, and duration. The bulk of focus group discussion in this area centered on technical training program experiences, with limited discussion about academic instruction among participants who were still working toward their high school diploma or equivalence.

In considering the implications of training program perceptions on overall program experience and satisfaction, it is worth noting the delineation that many participants made when discussing their training experience and other dimensions of the program experience. Participants often spoke distinctly about "training" and "Job ChalleNGe," framing "training" as their technical education coursework, training program, or academic experiences, and "Job ChalleNGe" as their residential experience. This distinction is likely facilitated by the structure of program delivery: Most participants receive their training from non–Job ChalleNGe staff, most commonly college faculty, on a college campus; by contrast, their residential experiences are largely at the Job ChalleNGe facility supervised by program-employed staff members.

Participants were able to articulate the value of the skills and credentials that they were earning in their training during Job ChalleNGe, noting the jobs or future training for which they were becoming qualified or how they might not have had access to this training otherwise. They spoke of the opportunities to earn a good wage and continue to grow their skills and qualifications through additional training and work experiences. One participant noted, "After I get out of here, I plan on going to a community college and getting more certifications in welding. I already have one from here. And hopefully after that, I'm going to start off at a fabrication shop so I can get some experience in welding so I can work for a contractor." Participants expressed gratitude for the opportunity to pursue such valuable training and, particularly, that it was free of charge to them and their families.

However, participants across sites noted that their training programs were too short to earn meaningful credentials. Job ChalleNGe's maximum length is five-and-a-half months, which in most of the training fields is not sufficient to qualify participants for the jobs to which they aspire.[7] When participants elaborated on this point, they discussed additional credentials or work experience that they needed to secure jobs. Accordingly, many participants said that they aspired or planned to pursue additional education and training in their fields after they completed Job ChalleNGe. We saw this reflected in the plans that participants indicated for their time after ChalleNGe. As shown in Table 3.3, 51 percent of partici-

---

[7] For additional discussion of findings related to misalignment between program length and credential or training program duration, see Wenger, Constant, et al., 2022.

pants intended to obtain a license or certificate in a career field, 19 percent intended to enroll in a bachelor's program, and 13 percent intended to enroll in an associate's degree program.[8]

Participants were able to articulate a number of potential career pathways, often leveraging the training they were receiving in Job ChalleNGe to pursue further training to qualify for military enlistment and secure desirable jobs. Consequently, their comments demonstrated an understanding that their Job ChalleNGe training was a starting point and that additional college credits or certifications would likely be advantageous or necessary to achieve their professional goals. In most cases where participants discussed continuing their studies, they mentioned enrolling for further training with the Job ChalleNGe education partner institutions or pursuing an apprenticeship or other on-the-job training with a union. Nonetheless, participants noted that additional time in the program might be beneficial because they needed an additional one to three months of training, depending on field of study, to secure the foundational credentials required for work in their field of training.

Participants discussed their instructors and how their instruction style, classroom activities (e.g., in construction, participants learn the different aspects of construction by building a small home together), and other support (e.g., mentoring, introductions to potential employers) were helping or hindering their development. Participants shared mixed perspectives on the instructional style of their training program instructors, noting a preference for hands-on instruction and work and some reluctance or challenges with assigned reading and less-applied work. According to one participant pursuing the welding program track, "The most annoying [coursework] was the digital part of welding. It took too long. I prepared to learn hands-on. During lecture, I fall asleep. If I'm in the shop and can see what they're doing, I learn faster." Participants in some training programs noted that they found the integration of hands-on work and career development connections helpful for future employment. For instance, participants were very positive about instructor-provided opportunities to visit or meet with employers during their training. Lastly, at one site, female participants in a historically male field noted that they experienced less support from their instructor than the male students in their training track. Our protocol did not systematically ask about potential sex-based discrimination, so we cannot make broad conclusions about participants' experiences of this nature; however, given the potential implications of this experience, we note it here.

Challenges

Participants also noted challenges with insufficient resources for instructional support and completion of assignments. In the classroom context, participants who had two instructors in their training programs reflected that it made a big difference in getting their questions answered in a timely fashion and getting attentive support in developing technical skills.

---

[8] Participants were given 13 options to choose from, and they were asked to select all that applied. Of those participants who indicated plans to further their education and training by obtaining a license or certificate in a career field or enrolling in a bachelor's or associate's degree program, 21 percent indicated pursuing more than one credential.

Participants who had only one instructor noted that it was sometimes difficult to get their questions answered or to get feedback on their progress. Outside the classroom, participants across fields and sites expressed that they were limited in their ability to do their work and reading by a lack of tutors or cadre who had knowledge in the technical field and, to compound that, not having access to computers or phones to look up the answers to their questions. For example, at one site, participants in welding, automotive, and construction programs reported struggling to understand the content they were receiving from their trades program because of limited access to books and resources. Because their field had specialized knowledge, participants said they did not feel that they could seek academic support from cadre or other staff. Without field-specific expertise in cadre or access to the technology to find answers for themselves or complete coursework, participants noted that they were unable to get questions answered outside the classroom and, in some cases, were unable to access course materials or take quizzes that instructors populated into course management software. Relatedly, some participants who were still working on their high school credential noted that they did not have enough study support or time for their upcoming testing because of having to divide their attention between their training coursework and preparation for the high school equivalency examination. Participants articulated that ChalleNGe staff vacancies and the limited numbers of site staff created a situation in which they had abundant downtime without sufficient support for their studying.

Services and Supports

In this section, we discuss the services that Job ChalleNGe sites provide to support participants in various domains as they complete their high school credential or training track and prepare for future success.[9] Job ChalleNGe participants begin the program with shared experiences as Youth ChalleNGe cadets, layered on varied educational backgrounds and life experiences. For many participants, traditional paths of schooling have not been amenable to their goals and talents, and they seek alternative paths to prepare for the workforce. Our analysis of participant focus group and staff interview data highlighted several ways that sites provide supports to promote participants' academic and technical development, physical and mental health, and career development.

Educational Resources

Job ChalleNGe sites promote academic development by providing additional study resources, such as dedicated tutoring hours, study halls, and classes on test-taking strategies and study skills. While sites approached the provision of educational resources differently, participants reported that these resources were, at times, limited by the availability of staff.

---

[9] There were other participants, not included in the 4 percent of focus group participants solely pursuing the HiSET, who were pursuing their high school equivalency concurrent with a training program.

In some circumstances, sites were able to provide subject-matter experts to tutor participants in their training fields. For instance, according to a staff member, "[While phlebotomy students] study, the nurse and coordinator are available to answer questions. Phlebotomy is a lot of bookwork, especially for someone with developing study skills. Having them in the classroom and having staff to keep them on task helped." Staff at other sites noted that tutors were hired with the expertise necessary to support participants. At some sites, there are staff members who are tasked with creating materials and additional opportunities for academic development. For instance, at one Job ChalleNGe site, there is an educational coordinator who uses course syllabi, textbooks, and presentation slides to develop supplemental study materials (e.g., flashcards, study guides) for participants; focus group participants from that site remarked that they had found them helpful. One site has participants in the phlebotomy training program teach material to staff through presentations to help reinforce their learning. Participants noted that this approach allows them to deepen their understanding of the subject matter, and staff remarked that the approach gives them valuable insights into participants' learning needs. At another site, participants in the emergency medical technician trade program used study groups, which enabled them to learn different perspectives and offer support and motivation for learning. Staff from another site reported that providing classes on test-taking strategies and study skills helped their participants succeed in their coursework.

Staff at some sites reported using educational games, prizes, and awards to promote engagement and educational achievement. At one site, staff and participants discussed how cadre reward participants who attend study hall with movie nights or popcorn. At another site, participants described earning "JC bucks" for cultivating positive study habits. "It really doesn't matter if you make a '100' instead of a '93.' What matters is how you show up to take the test, how you study for it," according to the staff member who started the JC bucks program. The JC bucks can be redeemed for prizes, such as bath bombs or candy. Participants reported enjoying these reward systems and being motivated to complete their work because of these methods.

Several sites have also allocated program resources to dedicated spaces, reference materials, and technology to be used during daily study periods. Staff spoke about the resources dedicated to these spaces and the way in which they are intended to support participants' engagement with their coursework. Nonetheless, some participants identified lack of access to these materials as a challenge to their technical development.

Participants' perceptions of their need for greater academic support aligned with staff reports of participant aspirations and preparedness. For instance, some Job ChalleNGe and educational partner staff advise participants on credit transfer and financial aid applications so that participants can pursue further education. At several Job ChalleNGe sites, staff also identified that participants arrive at Job ChalleNGe with a greater need for academic supports than historically was the case. At one of the pilot sites, staff indicated that in the initial years of the program, the majority of participants entered Job ChalleNGe with a high school diploma or equivalent credential. However, they now observe more participants arriving without having completed a high school credential. Staff attributed the decrease in participants' credential completion to a drop in program interest following the COVID-19 pandemic, resulting in lower average participant age and sites lowering their admissions standards to meet enrollment targets.

Staff reported that they identified services to meet participant needs and promote academic achievement; however, sites do not always have the personnel to execute these strategies. Because of staff vacancies, there are not always teachers or cadre available to transport participants to campus for additional study opportunities, to provide tutoring on site, or to monitor online coursework. Staff from one site found that they had adequate staff to supervise daily activities but not enough to have positive reward activities for participants. At another site, staff reported feeling that having more staff to support instruction during study halls would enhance participants' understanding by enabling them to tailor support to individual needs. As a result, staff with other responsibilities often step in, making it more difficult to fulfill the standard tasks of their job. Site leaders are prioritizing hiring more cadre and educational personnel to help alleviate scheduling issues.

Health Services

Job ChalleNGe sites offered a variety of services to meet the physical and mental health needs of Job ChalleNGe participants. For example, participants' physical health issues are generally handled by in-house nursing staff; some sites have contracts with outside health service providers for more-advanced care. Job ChalleNGe sites that are collocated with Youth ChalleNGe often share a nurse; in these cases, staff and participants report that the nurse's primary responsibility is to Youth ChalleNGe, so Job ChalleNGe participants get limited attention. Some sites have a second nurse or a contract or on-staff physician, and a few sites connect participants with medical services provided by their educational partners (e.g., the community college health center). In our discussions with participants, few of them provided their opinions on available health services, although one participant noted that they felt that Job ChalleNGe staff were suspicious of participants' claims of being sick.

Participants and staff both had more to share regarding mental health services, noting that these services are markedly less robust than physical health supports. Job ChalleNGe site staff reported providing access to mental health services using a dedicated on-site counselor (either staffed or contracted); providing access to the Youth ChalleNGe program counselor; connecting participants with education partner counseling services; or connecting participants to telehealth services. Staff stressed that Job ChalleNGe is not a therapeutic program for participants with serious mental health problems. While it is not the right program for individuals who need the "current, regular support of a psychiatrist," as one staff member put it, staff acknowledged that participants often have mental health conditions that need treatment and monitoring.

Counselors can provide structures and support to facilitate program operation and success. Staff from one site reported that their counselor does "a psychosocial intake assessment" that provides the counselor with "a baseline for things like substance abuse, mental health, and family dynamics" and notifies the staff about participants they "need to keep a closer eye on." Staff at another site commented that the staff counselor helps cadre and leadership keep track of participants with mental health challenges, relaying information back and forth to ensure that all staff are aware of any mental health developments. However, robust psychological counseling is not widely available across Job ChalleNGe programs. Sharing counseling staff with Youth ChalleNGe was not considered ideal by staff because it limits Job ChalleNGe participants' access to counseling. As with nurses, mental health counselors are typically staffed to Youth ChalleNGe; thus, Job ChalleNGe participants are second priority. Staff from a few sites reported that their site utilized their educational partners' mental health services, giving participants the opportunity to meet with counselors on the partner college campus.

In the focus groups, participants made it clear that they noticed the lack of available counseling and wanted more access to counselors. They described Job ChalleNGe as "not an easy experience," which can be compounded by the challenges from their home life and in their relations with peers in the program. Participants discussed experiencing stress from interactions with peers with whom they do not get along but are required to spend time; this can spur anger and affect their mental health. Given these challenges, participants shared that their sites needed access to additional mental health counselors on site, as there is often a long waiting list to see the counselor.

Unfortunately, sites can find it challenging to secure a counselor position, and, even when budgeted, the positions can be hard to fill. Staff and participants alike expressed that it is critical for Job ChalleNGe participants to have access to a qualified mental health professional for both acute and ongoing mental health support. A staff member at one site reported, "Counselors are needed to help [participants] cope with past trauma or care that may come up during the cycle." Another site's staff mentioned that mental health issues can also make it difficult to place participants in postprogram opportunities.

Career Services

All sites reported providing a variety of career services (e.g., career counseling, resume assistance, interview coaching, placement services) to prepare participants for postprogram opportunities. In our interviews and focus groups, both staff and participants described the different ways these services were delivered. These included incorporating a variety of activities to help participants learn about different career paths, develop soft skills, and apply for and secure jobs. Job ChalleNGe employment or placement coordinators play a central role in initiating and building relationships with employers, and staff from several sites described strong employer partnerships that were beneficial for placing participants into jobs. However, most sites did not appear to have a developed, long-term strategy for building relationships with employers. Site staff described multiple barriers to placement, including developing employer relationships, ensuring that participants' preparation meets employer requirements, and adequately supporting participants from career coaching through the application and interview process.

Career Exploration and Soft Skills

Staff at all sites reported that they help participants learn about careers, plan for their future careers, and develop the soft skills needed for employment. For instance, staff at four sites reported that participants complete a P-RAP, or graduate action plan, that specifies goals after graduation and the steps participants need to take to reach these goals.[10] Staff also described how training program instructors promoted participants' career exploration: Instructors help participants learn about career fields by bringing in guest speakers, providing workplace tours, describing their personal experience in the field, and providing a training environment that emulates a professional work environment.

To supplement professional development in their training tracks, most sites provide career development instruction on site. Four sites described providing structured courses or curricula that covered employment skills. For example, the "essential skills" class at one of the sites included communication skills and business ownership. Another site implemented a rewards program for participants who displayed professionalism and a strong work ethic. In addition, two of the sites provided work experience, including internships in the installation's dining facility and paid work at the Boys and Girls Club, which could help participants develop the soft skills needed for future employment.

Job Application Support

All sites provided activities to help participants apply for and secure jobs. Focus group participants most frequently mentioned receiving help with writing or updating resumes and engaging in mock interviews. Participants also, albeit less frequently, reported activities that helped them learn about potential careers and their salaries and how to conduct a job search, draft a cover letter, and complete job applications or W-2 forms. Some sites described creative activities to help participants apply for jobs and prepare for interviews. For example, one site used a role-playing game where participants played interviewers on a hiring panel. That site also had outside individuals conduct mock interviews. Another site introduced participants to the Department of Labor website and American Job Centers as sources of job information and required participants to apply for Job Corps, an education and vocational training program for individuals aged 16–24 that is administered by the Department of Labor. In addition to preparatory activities, staff at most sites mentioned that they provided material supports to help participants interview for jobs. Staff from two sites mentioned that the site would provide clothes for a job interview, and all other sites reported that staff would travel with a participant to interviews. Staff at one site said that job application skills were largely covered by Youth ChalleNGe, but that staff were available to help with these skills. Most sites also reported using some career services (e.g., counseling, placement) at their educational partners to supplement their offerings to participants.

---

[10] The P-RAP is a tool that is used by all Youth ChalleNGe sites to help cadets plan their futures; for more information, see Corte and Padilla, 2021.

All sites provided events and activities to connect participants with employers. Most sites reported that they used the staff placement counselor to help connect participants to employers. At these sites, placement counselors introduced participants to employers at job fairs and by hosting employers on site, provided recommendations, and helped arrange applications to apprenticeship programs. Staff at most sites mentioned job fairs, with staff at one site reporting that it both hosted a job fair on site and brought participants to job fairs off site.

Site staff and focus group participants suggested different levels of emphasis on activities to help participants apply for jobs or different levels of satisfaction with these activities. Participants at two sites expressed that the activities provided by the site were helpful and that they felt well prepared. In contrast, some of the participants at another site reported that help with interview preparation and resume writing had not been delivered consistently.

Outreach to Local Employers

All sites partner with local and regional employers to place Job ChalleNGe participants in jobs aligned with their field of study. Staff at most sites described employment or placement coordinators as playing a central role in initiating and building relationships with employers. Coordinators' roles were described as having three main functions: (1) finding jobs for participants by (2) identifying employers where participants might be placed and (3) informing the employers about Job ChalleNGe. The coordinator at one site explained that they used Google Maps and Facebook help-wanted groups to identify employers in the region that might employ trades provided by the site. The coordinator then called or sent brochures and flyers to employers to inform them about Job ChalleNGe. In addition to leveraging its placement coordinator, one site invited employers to meet participants and learn about Job ChalleNGe at student events, such as a building competition for participants in the construction program, graduation ceremonies, and barbecues. In addition, some sites use their associated foundations to facilitate connections to local employers.

While many staff reported that their employer partnerships were underdeveloped, staff at two sites described strong partnerships with employers. For example, one staff member described their site's partnership with a construction company: "We work hand in hand with them. They have their senior operators come and do personal interviews with our kids. If there are opportunities for jobs in that kid's home area, that kid is guaranteed a job interview." Sites also described partnerships with automotive servicing companies, a large chemical company, a local hospital, and unions that could hire participants in the construction trades. Staff at all sites described being in the process of building relationships with employers, most with an emphasis on employers with a statewide presence. Overall, staff described these partnerships as beneficial for placing participants into employment. According to the data call, local employers who have hired from Job ChalleNGe have provided sites with positive feedback on their graduates.

Although they described partnerships with employers, most sites did not appear to have carefully thought-out or long-term strategies for building relationships with employers. One site reported that it lacked a good marketing process, and another site reported that it needed a different strategy for placement, including updating training tracks so that they are more aligned with employer needs.

Interviews with staff suggest that the current training tracks offered are out of alignment with local employers' needs, creating a barrier to placement. Staff from several sites described efforts to update or adjust the trades they offered in response to market demand and student interests. For example, sites reported adding training or certifications in culinary arts, welding, drone operations, and restaurant management, as well as considering adjustments to existing tracks. Staff from some sites expressed a desire to add other trades but described barriers. For example, some staff described interest in adding automotive collision and repair and barber or cosmetology training. However, training providers for automotive collision and repair were unavailable in the local area, and barber or cosmetology training would require too many hours to complete within the Job ChalleNGe time frame.

Areas for Improvement

Staff generally reported being concerned about participants' postgraduation placement in jobs and other opportunities. In addition to cross-site concerns about alignment between placement and participants' training fields, two sites reported low placement rates. A staff member at one of these sites said that only one-quarter of participants were career and placement ready when they graduate. However, this staff person said that the program still served a valuable function by teaching participants they can handle demanding courses and encouraging graduates to consider postsecondary education (e.g., community college). Staff from both sites said Job ChalleNGe was not well known and that more marketing and partnerships were needed. By contrast, staff at other sites have begun to report positive placement outcomes with established employer partnerships and greater employer familiarity with Job ChalleNGe. This suggests that developing local employers' familiarity with the program and establishing more employer partnerships may help place participants into jobs at some sites. Staff across most sites reported needing more resources for developing relationships with employers. These resources included additional staff and funding for travel to meet employers.

Staff from several sites described requirements of employers as barriers to placement. Most sites reported that participants being younger than age 18 was a barrier to placement, and, in alignment with the participants' perceptions reported earlier, staff from most sites said that Job ChalleNGe was not long enough for participants to receive all the training or certification they would need for placement. In addition, one site reported that large companies often had too many requirements for placing participants.

At several sites, staff described needs for supports and services that may improve placement, namely transportation, addressing participants' basic needs, personal equipment required for employment, and substance use disorder resources. Two sites reported that they are more successful at placing participants in jobs that are local to the Job ChalleNGe site; however, their participants from other regions of the state do not have access to housing, transportation, or their support networks in the local area. A participant from one site shared, "[Staff] help us secure jobs. They have partners and sponsors that can help us secure jobs in our pathways. The only thing is that it may be in a location that we don't have transportation or housing." Across sites, participants encounter difficulty in securing housing after graduating due to their age and circumstances. In response to participant needs, one site worked with a nonprofit organization that provides housing, and another site helped graduates apply for public resources for housing, health care, and food to help them get on their feet while job searching and beginning to work after graduation. Through both interviews and the information request from Job ChalleNGe sites, transportation was consistently identified as an external barrier to participants securing jobs. Many Job ChalleNGe participants do not have a driver's license or access to a car or insurance; they also do not live in areas with robust public transportation systems. These factors limit the jobs to which a graduate can apply. Some sites provided help with earning a learner's permit or driver's license; however, the timing and logistics, coordination, and budget issues are barriers to the consistent provision of driver's education. Additionally, staff from one site said participants needed work uniforms and tools, which could be expensive. Finally, two sites reported that participants needed substance use disorder resources, which might be needed to ensure that participants are eligible for opportunities with employers that enforce a drug-free workplace policy.

Personal Development and Interpersonal Skills

Job ChalleNGe sites provide various opportunities for participants to cultivate their interpersonal skills. In staff interviews and participant focus groups, individuals shared perspectives on the current opportunities related to social engagement on site and personal development for participants. At some sites, participants were involved in "student government," which allowed participants to take on leadership roles and convene fellow participants to brainstorm and propose new activities for the community. At one site, participants discussed how their involvement in peer leadership taught them "how to guide and listen to one's peers." Some sites also incorporated a foundational course through their education partners that cultivates participants' emotional intelligence. According to participants from one site, "In 'Foundational Skills,' we learn life coping skills to deal with people who annoy you or who you get frustrated with." Participants at a few sites discussed how their involvement in Job ChalleNGe helped them gain a "new mindset" about working with others from different backgrounds or those with different personalities. At another site, participants shared how volunteer activities were opportunities for them to cultivate teamwork and collaboration.

Participants from several sites also acknowledged attending classes and activities that tended to their personal development. These classes promoted their financial literacy, with topics including managing money and budgeting, securing a credit card and building credit, and completing their tax returns. Participants also worked on time management and building their capacity to manage stress and their emotions through therapeutic activities, such as meditation and outdoor hikes.

Role of Education Partners

Education partners—local community colleges, adult education centers, and private institutes that provide students' technical training and other opportunities for development and support—play a meaningful role in the achievement and success of Job ChalleNGe participants. Education partners provide the academic opportunities for participants to secure the necessary knowledge and skills for their intended trade and can provide expanded services and resources for participants. These services and resources can include academic support, career development, health care, basic needs, and social engagement; most often, costs for these services are included in students' tuition, so there is no out-of-pocket cost for using them on an as-needed basis during the semester. These services can either address a resource gap or supplement existing resources available at Job ChalleNGe sites. Table 3.4 presents the number of sites that currently leverage their education partners for key services and resources, as reported in the data call. While one-half of all sites are benefiting from access to their education partners' health services, we see less use of their services and resources for career readiness and equipment access. Although it might be logistically complicated in terms of transportation and staffing, drawing more fully on these existing resources could be a boon to both participants and sites.

Our visits captured additional ways and a more detailed understanding of how education partners have played a key role in providing participants with what they need to succeed. As reported by one site, education partners provided participants with access to study labs, testing centers, tutorial services, and personal development courses. Study labs and tutorial services were crucial in providing participants off-site space to study and support with their studies. Job ChalleNGe sites can struggle with finding sufficient space to support the wide variety of participant needs. And while cadre, as reported in Wenger, Constant, and colleagues (2022), try to help participants with their studies, the support is often not effective because the topics are outside cadre's subject-matter expertise. Unfortunately, participants'

TABLE 3.4

Number of Sites Leveraging Education Partners, by Service and Resource

Service and Resource	Sites Drawing on Educational Partner Resource
Medical and health services	3
Mental and emotional counseling	2
Career counseling	1
Resume assistance	2
Interview coaching	2
Placement services	1
Computer access	1

use of available supports is not consistent because of the education partner's distance from the residential site and the difficulty of scheduling staff to chaperone participants to the education partner location. One site also shared how one of its education partners provided a life skills course to participants, thereby supplementing the activities and experiences participants receive on site to address the life coping skills component.

Services and supports to promote student well-being were reported by three sites. Staff from one site shared with us that their participants often access their education partner's health services and food pantry. The Job ChalleNGe site does provide medical services to participants on the residential site. However, participants have required medical services while on campus, and the availability of such services alleviated the need for Job ChalleNGe staff to transport participants back to the residential site. Moreover, participants have also taken advantage of the campus food pantry, which is a helpful resource if they are required to spend additional time on campus for their studies. Staff from another site also mentioned how their education partner invited their participants to campus events, providing participants with additional social outlets and an opportunity to experience college life.

Budgeting Priorities and Shortfalls

Job ChalleNGe staff from three sites indicated (1) sufficient personnel, (2) trade programs aligned with participant interests and goals, and (3) access to mental health services as the key considerations for allocating funds to support site operation. Staff from two sites shared that the bulk of their funding is dedicated to maintaining sufficient personnel. In the standardized information request, Job ChalleNGe leaders indicated that the cadre role has been particularly difficult to hire for because the salary range is not competitive with similar roles at other state and federal agencies; this, in addition to the lengthy hiring process, likely contributes to the low number of applications that sites receive for open vacancies.[11] While these sites would like to start cadre at a higher salary range, they are unable to because the salaries are set at the state level. As long as sites are unable to improve the competitiveness of the salaries for cadre, they will likely continue to experience disruption in program operations. According to staff from one site, "Our salaries are out of date. Until we raise them, we're going to have challenges with our staff." Put simply, if there are not sufficient cadre, participant activities are limited, likely affecting the experience that participants receive at Job ChalleNGe.

Sites are also exploring and offering driver's education on a pilot basis. Many of the trades that participants seek to enter require a driver's license for employment. Insufficient funds and staffing have prevented sites from providing this opportunity. As a result, employment options after Job ChalleNGe are limited for participants without a driver's license.

---

[11] Within Youth ChalleNGe sites, staff turnover is linked to lower graduation rates; turnover is higher and hiring is more difficult when starting salaries are lower and when other civilian wages are higher (Wenger et al., 2021; Wenger, Cottrell, and Wrabel, 2023).

Conclusion

In this chapter, we present findings that were drawn from a standardized information request and from staff interviews and participant focus groups. We discussed program implementation, including a focus on the residential experience; the training program and education partner supports; education, health, and career support services; and site funding priorities. According to our analyses, Job ChalleNGe sites work diligently to prepare participants for success during and after the program. It is clear, given the mission of Job ChalleNGe, that sites are providing participants with an academic or technical pathway forward, including several training tracks to choose from, room and board that provides structure to participants and allows them to stay focused on their career development, opportunities to develop their skills and capacity for seeking employment, and a team of staff charged with facilitating their experience and success. While this applies broadly to all six sites, challenges—both distinct and interconnected—continue to endure and hamper sites' ability to achieve the desired outcomes.

Job ChalleNGe participants arrive with a diverse variety of backgrounds and experiences. Site leadership and staff, with limited resources, develop and implement services, supports, and opportunities that speak to the vast diversity in participant background, circumstance, and education, but the challenges demonstrate that programs need additional resources to help participants fully meet the goals set forth by the Job ChalleNGe mission. Academic and career outcomes are affected by the opportunities and supports that participants are given to navigate the challenges—material, academic, and health—in their lives. Job ChalleNGe may not be intended or set up to address participants' mental health needs, as described by staff, but our findings suggest that sites *need* to be more responsive to the interconnected challenges that influence participants' experiences and outcomes to fulfill the Job ChalleNGe mission.

CHAPTER 4

Long-Term Outcomes for Youth and Job ChalleNGe Graduates in Georgia

Although the Youth ChalleNGe sites collect and report substantial amounts of data on participation and short-term outcomes, the sites are not directed or resourced to collect data on long-term outcomes (the logic model in Figure 1.1 details both short- and long-term outcome measures). Measuring long-term outcomes is necessary to determine the extent to which the ChalleNGe program is meeting its mission—producing graduates with the education, training, and skills to find success as productive citizens (see Chapter 1). Collecting data on long-term outcomes could be done by tracking graduates for several years after they leave the program or by matching ChalleNGe graduates' information to existing administrative databases.[1] State Longitudinal Data Systems (SLDSs) offer one option for matching ChalleNGe data to other administrative databases and tracking longer-term outcomes.

SLDSs are designed to help state policymakers make data-driven decisions. These systems combine administrative records from multiple sources, including records of all students in the state attending public prekindergarten through 12th grade schools, enrollment in postsecondary institutions, and state workforce participation and wages. What makes these data systems unique is that, unlike prior efforts in which data were available only at aggregate levels, SLDS data link individual-level information, allowing for rich analyses of long-term outcomes for specific groups of individuals. Of course, SLDSs are state-specific; therefore, measuring outcomes across ChalleNGe sites from different states requires accessing multiple databases. SLDS databases do not yet exist in every state; each state has slightly different requirements for the type of data that is stored in the system and how to access the data.[2]

To test the ability of the SLDSs to support an analysis of long-term outcomes for ChalleNGe graduates, we obtained access to one such database in a single state, Georgia. Georgia was selected because it includes a Job ChalleNGe site, has multiple Youth ChalleNGe sites, and has a three-decade history of ChalleNGe operating in the state—and because the SLDS data could be matched to ChalleNGe participants and then made available to researchers. Additionally, the SLDS includes both education and labor market data. There have been three

---

[1] For a more detailed discussion of long-term outcome measures and strategies for collecting the relevant data, see Wenger, Wrabel, et al., 2022.

[2] For more information about SLDS policies and resources, see Education Commission of the States, 2021.

Youth ChalleNGe sites in Georgia: Fort Eisenhower Youth ChalleNGe Academy (established in 2000),[3] Fort Stewart Youth ChalleNGe Academy (established in 1993), and Milledgeville Youth ChalleNGe Academy (which operated from 2016 until 2020). The Job ChalleNGe site opened at Fort Stewart in 2016.

Each ChalleNGe site collects information about cadets by class, with each site operating classes on different time frames for the five-month program (for example, historically, new classes started in March and September in Fort Eisenhower, and January and July in Fort Stewart). Working with the state leadership for Georgia's ChalleNGe programs and the Georgia Governor's Office of Student Achievement (GOSA), we were able to access data including deidentified information on all Georgia Youth and Job ChalleNGe participants and all other students enrolled in public schools in Georgia. Using these data, we sought to answer the following research questions:

1. What is the geographic distribution of the student population served by the Georgia Youth ChalleNGe programs?
2. How do the 8th-grade background characteristics, school behaviors, and academic achievement of Georgia Youth ChalleNGe and Job ChalleNGe graduates compare with non-ChalleNGe participants in Georgia?
3. How do the outcomes among Youth and Jobs ChalleNGe graduates compare with each other and non-ChalleNGe participants in Georgia?
4. What is the impact of Youth ChalleNGe on postsecondary and labor market outcomes?

Analysis Overview

We first examine the geographic distribution of the student population that is served by Georgia Youth and Job ChalleNGe programs. In this analysis, we take advantage of the statewide data over a ten-year period to understand to what extent the Georgia Youth ChalleNGe programs are recruiting from across the state in terms of the number of schools and districts that send at least one student to a Georgia Youth ChalleNGe program. This provides important context for understanding the findings of the other research questions and also provides a first look at the geographic distribution of recruitment efforts for the Youth ChalleNGe program.

Next, we describe the 8th-grade background characteristics, school behaviors, and academic achievement of Georgia Youth and Job ChalleNGe graduates compared with youth in the entire state. The purpose of this analysis is to examine how graduates from the two programs differ before entering the program in terms of their gender, race and ethnicity, participation in school programs, school behaviors, and academic achievement compared with

---

[3] Fort Eisenhower was formerly named Fort Gordon.

students in Georgia who did not participate in ChalleNGe. We hypothesized that we would find significant differences across many of the measures and that graduates from the two programs would be more disadvantaged than the average student from Georgia.

We also describe the long-term outcomes for Youth and Job ChalleNGe graduates, comparing the outcomes of Youth ChalleNGe graduates with the outcomes of Job ChalleNGe graduates and comparing the outcomes of both of these groups with the outcomes of other students who attended public school in Georgia but did not participate in the program. We compare outcomes between Youth ChalleNGe and Job ChalleNGe in this step because the Job ChalleNGe program is intended to help participants pursue locally in-demand job certificates, and we therefore hypothesized that youth completing this program will have higher rates of obtaining these certificates. The outcomes for this analysis include enrollment in a two-year institution, attainment of certificates and associate's degrees, labor market participation, and annual wages. This descriptive analysis is an important first step in examining outcome differences, but it does not account for the selection process of the program or any differences in background characteristics.

Finally, we examine the impact of the Youth ChalleNGe program on long-term outcomes using a propensity score weighting regression methodology.[4] This quasi-experimental research design compares outcomes for Youth ChalleNGe program graduates with outcomes for youth who have observably similar backgrounds but who did not participate in ChalleNGe. The purpose of this analysis is to account for the selection process and determine whether the Youth ChalleNGe program is affecting outcomes.

Data Sources

This analysis combines data from the Georgia's Academic and Workforce Analysis and Research Data System, which is the state's prekindergarten through workforce longitudinal data system, GA•AWARDS, with cadet-level information from three Georgia Youth ChalleNGe sites and the Georgia Job ChalleNGe site. The ChalleNGe sites shared identifying information about cadets and participation/graduation data with GOSA. GOSA staff matched the cadet data with GA•AWARDS data, removed identifying information, and then provided the linked data to the research team.

The GA•AWARDS data we analyze span from school year (SY) 2010–2011 through 2018–2019.[5] These individual-level data files allow us to track youth as they progress through the public K–12 school system into postsecondary education or the workforce. The files include demographic and background characteristics, scores on state standardized assessments,

---

[4] The relatively short history of Job ChalleNGe and the window of SLDS data available mean that it is not yet possible to track outcomes for Georgia Job ChalleNGe participants on long-term outcomes (those occurring more than seven years after graduation).

[5] Education information from GA•AWARDS is recorded based on school years (e.g., SY 2016 refers to the 2015–2016 school year, which began in July/August 2015 and ended in May 2016).

schools attended, reasons for leaving a school, enrollment in postsecondary education, high school and postsecondary completion status and certificates obtained, and quarterly wages. Detailed information about how we define measures based on the data is described in the following sections. Additional information on these data is available in Appendix B.

Analytic Methods

We use a combination of descriptive and regression analysis to answer our research questions. Our first two questions summarize the geographic distribution of Youth ChalleNGe cadets across the state of Georgia and how similar Youth and Job ChalleNGe participants are to students in Georgia who did not participate in ChalleNGe. Our third question focuses on comparing the observed long-term outcomes for Youth and Job ChalleNGe graduates with each other and with students in Georgia who did not participate in ChalleNGe. Finally, we use propensity score weighting regression analysis to estimate the effect of ChalleNGe on long-term outcomes for our fourth research question. In the following sections, we describe our methods. Additional details on these methods are provided in Appendix B.

Descriptive Analysis of Geographic Distribution of Youth ChalleNGe Cadets

The GA•AWARDS files allow us to examine the distribution of Youth ChalleNGe cadets across schools in the state. For this research question, we summarize the number and percentage of schools and districts that have students who enroll in Youth ChalleNGe, the average number of students who typically participate in Youth ChalleNGe from a given school over the nine SYs covered by our data, and the characteristics of schools that have Youth ChalleNGe participants. This exploration is important for understanding the extent to which the analyses we present in this chapter are representative of the entire state.

Descriptive Analysis of Background Characteristics

For the second research question, we use two-sample, two-tailed *t*-tests, a statistical technique, to determine whether the groups are statistically equivalent on background characteristics. We conduct two sets of analyses to answer this research question. First, we test whether the average value of the measure is different between Youth ChalleNGe graduates compared with all students in Georgia. Second, we test whether the average value is different between Job ChalleNGe graduates compared with all students in Georgia.

The analysis for the second research question uses data on students' background characteristics measured when the youth are in 8th grade. While we have multiple measures of these characteristics because of the longitudinal nature of the data, using information from 8th grade ensures that the measurement occurs prior to the opportunity to participate in the Youth or Job ChalleNGe program, thereby capturing these characteristics at baseline. Demographic characteristics include gender and race and ethnicity. We also examine background characteristics, such as indicators for the student being low-income (as designated by the student being eligible for free or reduced-price lunch [FRPL]), whether a student is identified as an English learner student (ELS), students attending gifted programs, students with disabilities (SWD), and students experiencing homelessness (SEH). We examine continuous measures of grade 8 behaviors, such as the number of days the student was suspended in and out of school and the number of days the student was absent. Lastly, we examine two state standardized test scores: 8th-grade math scores and 8th-grade English/language arts (ELA) scores.

Descriptive Analysis of Long-Term Outcomes

The third research question also uses two-sample, two-tailed t-tests to test for differences among the populations. In this case, we conduct three sets of comparisons. First, we test whether there is a difference between Youth ChalleNGe graduates compared with Job ChalleNGe graduates. Then we test whether there is a difference in Youth ChalleNGe graduates compared with all students in Georgia and in Job ChalleNGe graduates compared with all students in Georgia. As mentioned earlier, we wish to compare outcomes between Youth ChalleNGe and Job ChalleNGe because the Youth ChalleNGe program is more focused on high school credit recovery, whereas the Job ChalleNGe program is intended to help participants pursue locally in-demand job certificates, and therefore we may see differences in these outcomes.

The outcomes examined under the third research question include education outcomes (measures of postsecondary enrollment and postsecondary completion) and labor market outcomes (workforce participation and earnings, which are measured as annual wages).[6] For education outcomes, we examine indicators of whether the youth enrolls in a two-year postsecondary institution, receives a postsecondary certificate (a technical certificate in an area of specialization, typically awarded to students who complete 30 or fewer credits), or earns an associate's degree (awarded for completing 60 credits of postsecondary education).[7]

Because we are able to follow the same individual over time in our data, we needed to identify the time frame in which to measure education outcomes. We began by placing youth into cohorts according to the year they attend eighth grade because this is the last year before students had the opportunity to attend Youth ChalleNGe. We then identified the years in which we could observe in our data whether youth were attending Youth ChalleNGe. Table 4.1 shows the 8th-grade cohorts for our sample (represented by a column in the table) and indicates the SYs in which we can observe in our data that the youth could have attended Youth ChalleNGe (shaded). For example, youth who were in 8th grade in SY 2013 (the fourth

---

[6] The GA•AWARDS data also include a measure of total earnings, defined as the sum of *all* recorded earnings in Georgia to date. This measure also exists for every year. We complete parallel analyses on this measure; the results were similar to those found when we examined annual wages. We include descriptive statistics on this variable in Appendix B.

[7] While we had hoped to include as one of the outcomes whether the youth obtains a high school degree or equivalent, we were not able to do so due to data limitations. While GA•AWARDS data contain information on whether the student obtained a high school diploma or passed the GED subject tests, the data do not contain information about the HiSET, a GED assessment alternative that is commonly taken by Georgia Youth ChalleNGe cadets and graduates. Without data on the HiSET, we are not able to calculate the true high school equivalent attainment rate for program participants (and nonparticipants), and therefore we cannot examine the effect of the program on this outcome.

TABLE 4.1

Cohorts of 8th-Grade Students Across School Years in the Analysis File

SY	8th-Grade Cohort			
	2011	2012	2013	2014
2011	8th			
2012	9th	8th		
2013	10th	9th	8th	
2014	11th	10th	9th	8th
2015	12th	11th	10th	9th
2016	Freshman	12th	11th	10th
2017	Sophomore	Freshman	12th	11th
2018	Junior	Sophomore	Freshman	12th
2019	Senior	Junior	Sophomore	Freshman

column of the table) could have participated in Youth ChalleNGe in SY 2014, SY 2015, SY 2016, or SY 2017.[8] Note that for the 2011 cohort, we cannot observe cadets in 2012 because cadet-level data collection did not start in Georgia until 2013. The cell labels display the grade level for youth following a typical grade progression across SYs, including their seniority in college (e.g., "freshman"). For each cohort of 8th-grade students, we have a different number of years in which we are able to measure long-term education outcomes, given that the data from GA•AWARDS end in 2019.

We measure all education outcomes relative to 8th-grade completion. For example, most students graduate from high school four years after enrolling in 8th grade. If a student followed a standard grade progression, they would be expected to enroll in postsecondary education within five years of when they started 8th grade. However, not all students complete high school in four years, and not all students directly enroll in postsecondary education. To account for varying timelines, we measure whether each outcome was obtained based on both a standard grade progression and allowing for additional time. The number of additional years at which we assess each outcome was determined by the number of years for which we have data and can observe each outcome. Table 4.2 shows education outcome measures and the 8th-grade cohorts for whom we could observe these outcomes.

---

[8] The 2015–2019 cohorts of 8th-grade students are dropped from the analysis of outcomes, which includes any cadet who enrolled in the program between 2015 and 2019. This is because we do not have sufficient data to observe students obtaining the long-term outcomes of interest because our data from GA•AWARDS end with SY 2019.

TABLE 4.2

Education Outcomes and 8th-Grade Cohorts

Outcome Measure	8th-Grade Cohorts
Enrollment in two-year institution, within 5 years	2011, 2012, 2013, 2014
Enrollment in two-year institution, within 6 years	2011, 2012, 2013
Enrollment in two-year institution, within 7 years	2011, 2012
Enrollment in two-year institution, within 8 years	2011
Certificate, within 6 years	2011, 2012, 2013
Certificate, within 7 years	2011, 2012
Certificate, within 8 years	2011
Associate's degree, within 6 years	2011, 2012, 2013
Associate's degree, within 7 years	2011, 2012
Associate's degree, within 8 years	2011

NOTE: *Within x years* refers to the time frame since someone's first 8th-grade attendance in the Georgia public school system. For example, if someone attended 8th grade in 2011, they were counted as enrolled in a two-year institution within five years if they enrolled by 2016 or earlier.

The third research question also examines differences in labor market outcomes. Our labor market measures include an indicator of whether the youth enters the labor force in Georgia, as well as measures of annual wages in Georgia between the ages of 18 and 24 (after completing the ChalleNGe program, where applicable).[9] The analysis sample for the labor force outcomes also requires defining cohorts. In this case, however, we are not constrained by SYs because the labor force data in GA•AWARDS are provided annually. Therefore, we define cohorts of youth based on their age. Because date of birth is personally identifiable information that we are not permitted to access, we use the year that individuals attend 8th grade as a proxy for being age 13–14 as a starting point and calculate age based on the years after 8th grade.

Impact Analysis of the Youth ChalleNGe Program

For the fourth research question, we are interested in understanding the impact of Youth ChalleNGe on long-term outcomes. The gold-standard method of estimating the impact of a program is to use random assignment. However, during the period under study, youth were not randomly assigned to the Youth ChalleNGe program. Instead, youth were selected into the program based on recruitment activities by the program and needs of the student for ser-

---

[9] Labor force participation and quarterly wages available in GA•AWARDS are for people who work in Georgia for employers that provide wage data to the Georgia Department of Labor. This does not include wages earned in out-of-state jobs, by independent contractors, or by federal or military employees. We discuss the limitations of these data later.

vices. Because there is no single group of students in Georgia who can easily serve as a comparison to Youth ChalleNGe participants, we use statistical methods to identify an appropriate comparison group.

To estimate the impact of the Youth ChalleNGe program, we use a propensity score weighting regression analysis (see Appendix B for more details on this methodology). This approach enables us to generate an equivalent comparison group against which we can compare outcomes of Youth ChalleNGe graduates and is estimated in two steps.[10] In the first step, we estimate propensity score weights, which are determined using student characteristics measured in 8th grade. The controls in this weighting model include the background characteristics, participation in school programs, academic achievement, absences, and discipline measures we described under research question 2. They also include school-level averages of these characteristics to account for school contextual factors that may affect participation in the program and a set of indicator variables for the Regional Education Service Agency in which the school is located, which we use as a proxy for the region in the state where the youth attended 8th grade (Georgia Department of Education, undated).[11] The characteristics and behaviors measured before program participation allow us to form a weighted comparison group that is statistically similar to Youth ChalleNGe graduates. In the second step, we estimate the impact of Youth ChalleNGe on postsecondary and workforce outcomes using a regression with the weights created in step 1. This model regresses the outcome of interest (under research question 2) on measures of background characteristics, participation in school programs, academic achievement, absences, and discipline, applying sampling weights estimated in the first step.

This analytic approach allows us to estimate the causal impact of ChalleNGe because it provides comparison students that are much more similar to Youth ChalleNGe graduates (as measured by characteristics in 8th grade) than in the simple comparison presented in research question 2. Although the comparison group may be different in unobservable characteristics, we expect that balancing on observable characteristics increases the likelihood that unobservable characteristics are also similar (Li, Morgan, and Zaslavsky, 2018). This is particularly true if the unobservable characteristics that relate to program participation and outcomes, such as motivation to succeed, are correlated with the combination of observable characteristics (e.g., race, socioeconomic status, and test scores) we use in the models.

---

[10] While we had hoped to conduct a similar analysis with Job ChalleNGe graduates, the length of our panel and the small sample size of graduates prevented the weighting models from converging and producing weights that, when applied, result in comparison groups that are similar to the treatment group. As a result, the analysis in research question 4 is restricted to Youth ChalleNGe graduates.

[11] The 16 Regional Education Service Agencies in Georgia are regional education agencies that provide professional development and school improvement support and implement statewide education initiatives.

Analytic Samples

First, we present information about the number of participants in the Georgia ChalleNGe programs. Table 4.3 shows the number of Youth and Job ChalleNGe graduates by ChalleNGe graduation year in our analysis sample. We are not able to include all of these graduates in our analysis for a few reasons. First, when the ChalleNGe sites sent information to GOSA, there were 1,388 youth in the ChalleNGe files who could not be located in the GA•AWARDS data. In addition, for some of our analysis, we focus on student information measured in 8th grade, and some youth cannot be observed in our files because they are not attending public schools in Georgia at that grade level.

For the analysis of our first two research questions, we combine students across SY 2013–2014 and SY 2018–2019. For research question 2, the analytic sample differs depending on the characteristics we analyze. Table 4.4 shows the analytic sample sizes for the analysis for research question 2, separately for the analysis of demographic characteristics, background characteristics measured in grade 8, and test scores.

TABLE 4.3

Number of Youth and Job ChalleNGe Graduates in Georgia, by School Year

	Number of Graduates	
SY	Youth ChalleNGe	Job ChalleNGe
2014	874	N/A
2015	828	N/A
2016	814	92
2017	755	82
2018	870	86
2019	821	99
Total	4,962	359

NOTE: The table lists Youth and Job ChalleNGe graduates who are included in any of the analyses. N/A = not applicable.

TABLE 4.4

Sample Sizes for Background Characteristics

Characteristics	Youth ChalleNGe Graduates	Job ChalleNGe Graduates	Students in Georgia
Demographic characteristics	4,533	421	1,670,216
Grade 8 background characteristics	4,054	375	1,008,540
Grade 8 math test scores	3,778	350	904,198
Grade 8 ELA test scores	3,846	361	965,110

NOTE: Demographic characteristics include gender and race and ethnicity; grade 8 background characteristics include FRPL, SEH, SWD, ELS, and gifted.

Analysis Samples for Long-Term Outcomes

As described previously, the analytic samples for education and labor market outcomes depend on the number of cohorts of students for whom we can observe that outcome for the given time frame. Table 4.5 summarizes the sample sizes we use in the analysis of each outcome measure for research questions 3 and 4. Table 4.6 shows the sample sizes for Georgia labor force outcomes.

TABLE 4.5

Education Outcomes, Cohorts, and Sample Sizes

Outcome Measure	Cohorts Included	Sample Size
Enrollment in two-year institution, within 5 years	2011, 2012, 2013, 2014	378,992
Enrollment in two-year institution, within 6 years	2011, 2012, 2013	282,067
Enrollment in two-year institution, within 7 years	2011, 2012	186,477
Enrollment in two-year institution, within 8 years	2011	91,659
Certificate, within 6 years	2011, 2012, 2013	282,067
Certificate, within 7 years	2011, 2012	186,477
Certificate, within 8 years	2011	91,659
Associate's degree, within 6 years	2011, 2012, 2013	282,067
Associate's degree, within 7 years	2011, 2012	186,477
Associate's degree, within 8 years	2011	91,659

NOTE: *Within x years* refers to the time frame since someone's first 8th-grade attendance in the Georgia public school system.

TABLE 4.6

Labor Force Outcomes and Sample Sizes

Outcome Measure	Sample Size
Labor force participation at age 17–18	625,069
Labor force participation at age 18–19	494,880
Labor force participation at age 19–20	367,240
Labor force participation at age 20–21	242,246
Labor force participation at age 21–22	118,907
Annual wage at age 17–18	303,514
Annual wage at age 18–19	256,703
Annual wage at age 19–20	191,646
Annual wage at age 20–21	125,219
Annual wage at age 21–22	61,799

Results

What Is the Distribution of Youth ChalleNGe Cadets Across Schools in Georgia?

Over the ten-year period covered by our data and of the 1,113 middle and high schools in Georgia, we found that 54.7 percent of schools had at least one student who enrolled in Youth ChalleNGe. Georgia has 181 school districts (a vast majority of which have fewer than five schools); we found that 76 percent of school districts had at least one student who enrolled in Youth ChalleNGe. The districts that did not have any youth who enrolled in the program are small, with at most three schools. Overall, this examination of the distribution of students across schools and school districts reveals that the Youth ChalleNGe program draws students widely from across the state.

When we examine the number of youth who participated in the program across the ten-year period, we find that 23.6 percent of schools had one participant, 54.4 percent of schools had between one and five participants, and 67.4 percent of schools had between one and ten participants. Typically, once a school sent a participant in one year, it continued to send participants in subsequent years. Of schools that sent at least one participant, 58 percent of schools sent participants in three or more years.

When we examine the characteristics of schools with at least one Youth ChalleNGe participant compared with schools with no participants, we find few differences. We see that schools with at least one participant have a higher percentage of Black students, larger school enrollments, and students with a higher number of unexcused absences (see Table B.1 in Appendix B). Overall, we find that schools that send students to Youth ChalleNGe are very similar to schools with no participants.

How Do the 8th-Grade Background Characteristics and Behaviors of Youth ChalleNGe and Job ChalleNGe Graduates Compare with Non-ChalleNGe Graduates in Georgia?

Figure 4.1 shows the background characteristics of Youth and Job ChalleNGe graduates and other students in Georgia measured when the student is in 8th grade.[12] Overall, Youth and Job ChalleNGe graduates have a similar demographic makeup to one another. Youth ChalleNGe graduates are 21 percent female, 70 percent Black, 6 percent Latino, and 20 percent White (with other racial and ethnic categories coded separately, but not reported). About 82 percent of Youth ChalleNGe graduates come from low-income backgrounds (as denoted by receiving FRPL), 3 percent have experienced homelessness (SEH), 20 percent are SWD, 2 percent are ELS, and 2 percent are in the gifted program.

---

[12] Table B.1 in Appendix B presents this same information in a table format but also includes statistical testing to show which differences are statistically significant. In this section, we discuss only differences that are statistically significant.

As shown in Figure 4.1, the 8th-grade demographic characteristics and behaviors of Youth ChalleNGe graduates differ significantly from the characteristics of students in Georgia as a whole. Youth ChalleNGe graduates are less likely to be female (by 28 percentage points), more likely to be Black (by 32 percentage points), less likely to be Latino (by 6 percentage points), and less likely to be White (by 23 percentage points) than all public school students in Georgia. Youth ChalleNGe graduates are also more likely to be economically disadvantaged, with a higher percentage of Youth ChalleNGe graduates designated as low-income (by 22 percentage points), a higher percentage experiencing homelessness (by 1 percentage point), and a higher percentage having disabilities (by 8 percentage points). Youth ChalleNGe graduates are less likely to be ELS (by 1 percentage point) and are less likely to be enrolled in the gifted program compared with students in the state (by 11 percentage points).

Similarly, Figure 4.1 shows that the 8th-grade demographic characteristics of Job ChalleNGe graduates differ significantly from the characteristics of students in Georgia as a

FIGURE 4.1

Demographic Characteristics of Youth and Job ChalleNGe Graduates Compared with Students in Georgia

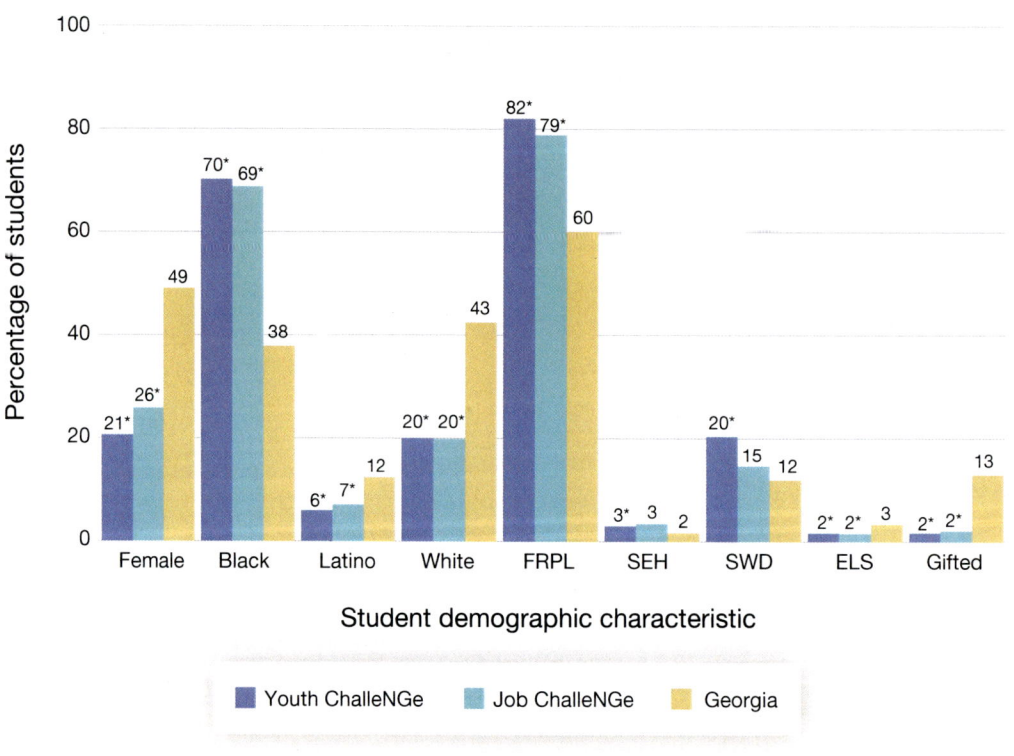

NOTE: Information for FRPL, SEH, SWD, ELS, and gifted was measured during grade 8 for each student. The sample consists of students whose most recent K–12 enrollment record indicates high school attendance, omitting students who had not yet attended high school by 2019. See Table B.1 in Appendix B for tests of statistical significance. Asterisks indicate instances where the difference between the Youth or Job ChalleNGe average characteristic is significantly different from the average characteristic for all public school students in Georgia ($p < 0.05$).

whole. Job ChalleNGe graduates are less likely to be female (by 23 percentage points), more likely to be Black (by 31 percentage points), less likely to be Latino (by 5 percentage points), and less likely to be White (by 23 percentage points) than all public school students in Georgia. Job ChalleNGe graduates are also more likely to be economically disadvantaged, with a higher percentage designated as low-income (by 19 percentage points). Job ChalleNGe graduates are slightly less likely to be ELS (by 1 percentage point) and less likely to be enrolled in the gifted program (by 11 percentage points) compared with public school students in the state.

We also examined school absences and disciplinary incidents (see Figure 4.2). We found that Youth ChalleNGe graduates were absent 6 percent of the time and Job ChalleNGe graduates were absent 4 percent of the time during their 8th-grade SY. In 8th grade, 47 percent of Youth ChalleNGe graduates and 43 percent of Job ChalleNGe graduates had at least one in-school suspension, and 41 percent of Youth ChalleNGe graduates and 33 percent of Job ChalleNGe graduates had at least one out-of-school suspension.

FIGURE 4.2

Absences and Disciplinary Outcomes of Youth and Job ChalleNGe Graduates Compared with Students in Georgia

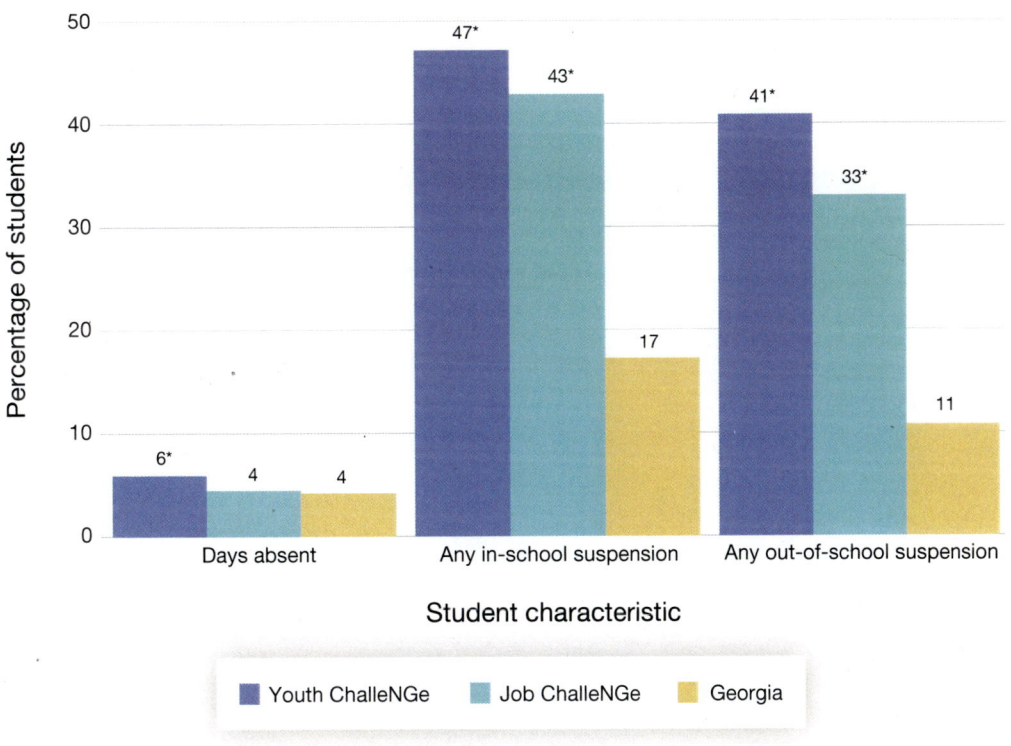

NOTE: Information about absence and suspensions is measured in grade 8. The sample for this plot consists of students whose most recent K–12 enrollment record indicates high school attendance, omitting students who had not yet attended high school by 2019. Asterisks indicate instances where the difference between the Youth or Job ChalleNGe average characteristic is significantly different from the average characteristic for all public school students in Georgia ($p < 0.05$).

Figure 4.2 also shows that there is a significant difference in absences and disciplinary outcomes for Youth and Job ChalleNGe graduates compared with all public school students in Georgia. Youth ChalleNGe graduates have more absences (by 2 percentage points) compared with all public school students in the state. Both Youth and Job ChalleNGe graduates are many times more likely to have in-school suspensions (by 30 and 26 percentage points, respectively) and out-of-school suspensions (by 30 and 22 percentage points, respectively) compared with students in the state.

Finally, we examined 8th-grade academic achievement in math and ELA. Because the test scores are standardized using data from the whole state, the standardized test scores for Georgia (denoted by the yellow bar) are normalized to 0. Figure 4.3 demonstrates that Youth and Job ChalleNGe graduates perform significantly worse on state math and ELA standardized tests than the typical student in Georgia. The average 8th-grade math standardized test score is −0.75 standard deviations for Youth ChalleNGe graduates and −0.63 standard deviations for Job ChalleNGe graduates. Similarly, the average 8th-grade ELA standardized test score is

FIGURE 4.3

Academic Achievement of Youth and Job ChalleNGe Graduates Compared with Students in Georgia

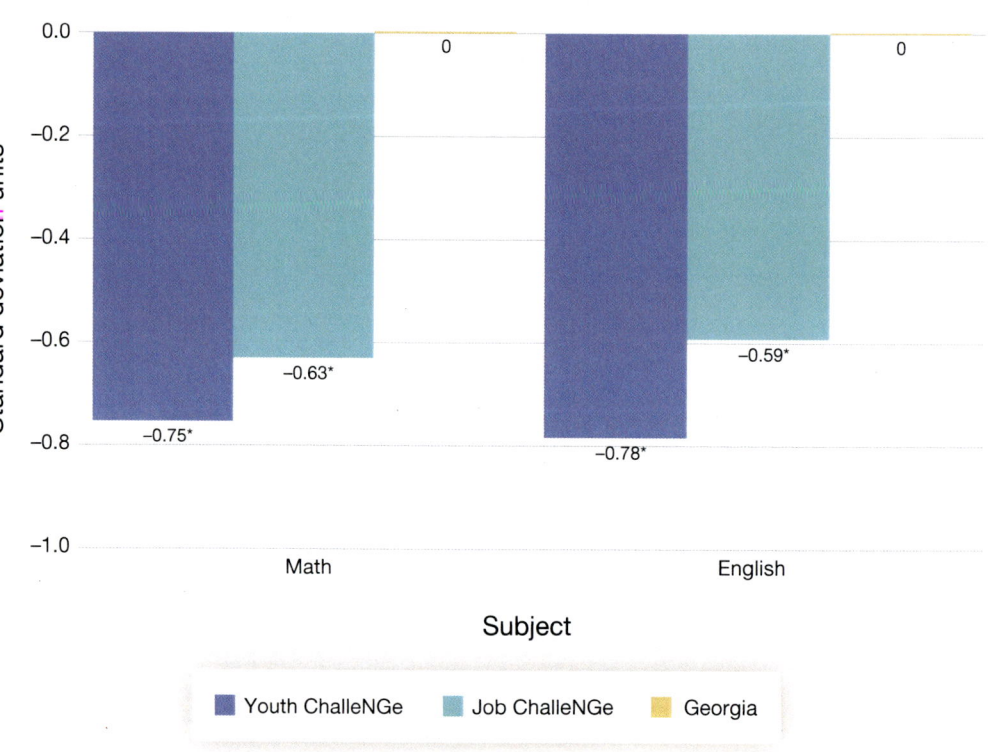

NOTE: The heights of the bars represent students' 8th-grade test scores in standard deviation units. Asterisks indicate instances where the difference between the Youth or Job ChalleNGe average characteristic is significantly different from the average characteristic for all public school students in Georgia ($p < 0.05$).

−0.78 standard deviations for Youth ChalleNGe graduates and −0.59 standard deviations for Job ChalleNGe graduates. For both subjects, Youth ChalleNGe graduates' scores are lower than Job ChalleNGe graduates' scores; however, both groups' scores are notably low, demonstrating that Youth and Job ChalleNGe graduates are struggling academically in 8th grade.[13]

How Do the Outcomes Among Youth and Job ChalleNGe Participants Compare with Each Other and Non-ChalleNGe Graduates in Georgia?

Next, we analyzed the postsecondary and labor market outcomes of Youth and Job ChalleNGe graduates relative to each other and relative to non-ChalleNGe graduates. Table 4.7 displays the rates of postsecondary enrollment and degree attainment for Youth and Job ChalleNGe graduates and whether the difference between the two groups is statistically significant. For postsecondary enrollment, we see that Youth ChalleNGe graduates enroll at a rate of 17–19 percent, whereas Job ChalleNGe graduates enroll in two-year institutions at much higher rates, 64–74 percent. These differences are large and statistically significant. A similar pattern is observed for obtaining certificates, with low rates for Youth ChalleNGe graduates (4–5 percent) and higher rates for Job ChalleNGe graduates (34–44 percent), and

TABLE 4.7

Youth and Job ChalleNGe Graduate Postsecondary Enrollment and Attainment

Outcome	Youth ChalleNGe (%)	Job ChalleNGe (%)	Difference (percentage points)
Enrollment in two-year institution, within 5 years	17	64	47*
Enrollment in two-year institution, within 6 years	18	74	56*
Enrollment in two-year institution, within 7 years	19	72	53*
Enrollment in two-year institution, within 8 years	18	N/A	N/A
Certificate, within 6 years	5	44	39*
Certificate, within 7 years	4	34	30*
Certificate, within 8 years	5	N/A	N/A
Associate's degree, within 6 years	0	0	0
Associate's degree, within 7 years	0	0	0
Associate's degree, within 8 years	0	0	0

NOTE: *Within x years* refers to the time frame since someone's first 8th-grade attendance in the Georgia public school system. Asterisks indicate instances where the difference between Youth and Job ChalleNGe is statistically significant at $p < 0.05$. N/A indicates not applicable; there were fewer than 10 graduates in the cell, and data are therefore suppressed.

---

[13] We examined whether these changes vary over time and found that the differences reported for the overall sample are consistent in each year of data.

the differences are again large and statistically significant. Youth and Job ChalleNGe graduates do not obtain associate's degrees in our sample time frame.

Comparing the labor market outcomes in Georgia for Youth and Job ChalleNGe graduates (see Table 4.8), we see that they participate in the labor force at similar rates (measured across all years of the panel), with 81–91 percent of Youth ChalleNGe graduates and 77–91 percent of Job ChalleNGe graduates participating. Annual wages for Youth ChalleNGe graduates are overall lower than those of Job ChalleNGe graduates until age 20–21, when the trend is reversed. Statistical tests reveal that the differences in these measures between Youth ChalleNGe and Job ChalleNGe participants are not statistically significant and thus may have occurred by chance.

We also compare the postsecondary and labor market outcomes for Youth and Job ChalleNGe graduates with youth attending public schools in Georgia. Overall, as seen in Figure 4.4, enrollment of Job ChalleNGe graduates in two-year institutions is much higher than enrollment by all students in Georgia. These differences remain consistent as the time frame for measuring enrollment increases, and they are statistically significant in each case. Youth ChalleNGe graduate enrollment in two-year institutions is similar to the state average.

TABLE 4.8
Youth and Job ChalleNGe Graduate Labor Market Outcomes

Outcome	Youth ChalleNGe	Job ChalleNGe	Difference
Labor force participation at age 17–18 (%)	81	77	4
Labor force participation at age 18–19 (%)	87	86	1
Labor force participation at age 19–20 (%)	80	91	2
Labor force participation at age 20–21 (%)	90	91	1
Labor force participation at age 21–22 (%)	91	N/A	N/A
Annual wage at age 17–18 ($)	6,364	6,343	21
Annual wage at age 18–19 ($)	8,832	9,916	−1,084
Annual wage at age 19–20 ($)	10,876	11,535	−659
Annual wage at age 20–21 ($)	13,147	11,664	1,482
Annual wage at age 21–22 ($)	12,781	N/A	N/A

NOTE: Labor market outcomes measured in the state of Georgia. Asterisks indicate instances where the difference between Youth and Job ChalleNGe is statistically significant at $p < 0.05$. N/A indicates not applicable; there were fewer than 10 graduates in the cell, and data are therefore suppressed.

FIGURE 4.4

Enrollment in Two-Year Institution of Youth and Job ChalleNGe Graduates Compared with Students in Georgia

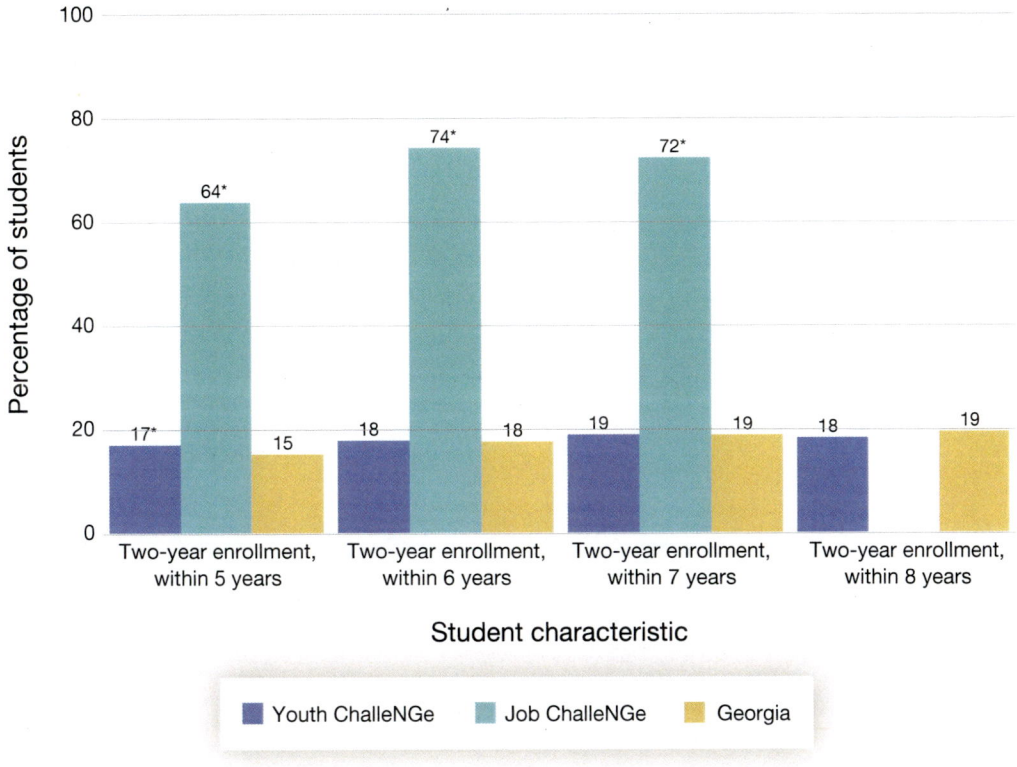

NOTE: *Within x years* refers to the time frame since someone's first 8th-grade attendance in the Georgia public school system. We suppressed the Job ChalleNGe results in the "Two-year enrollment, within 8 years" category because of sample size restrictions. Asterisks indicate instances where the difference between the Youth or Job ChalleNGe average characteristic is significantly different from the average characteristic for all public school students in Georgia ($p < 0.05$).

We present the average certificate attainment and associate's degree attainment for the three samples in Figure 4.5. The certificate attainment rate is much higher for Job ChalleNGe graduates compared with the state, with statistically significant differences of 41–30 percentage points, whereas the differences between Youth ChalleNGe graduates and the state average are not statistically significant. Associate's degree attainment is low for all students in Georgia, even within eight years of 8th-grade completion.

FIGURE 4.5

Postsecondary Credentials of Youth and Job ChalleNGe Graduates Compared with Students in Georgia

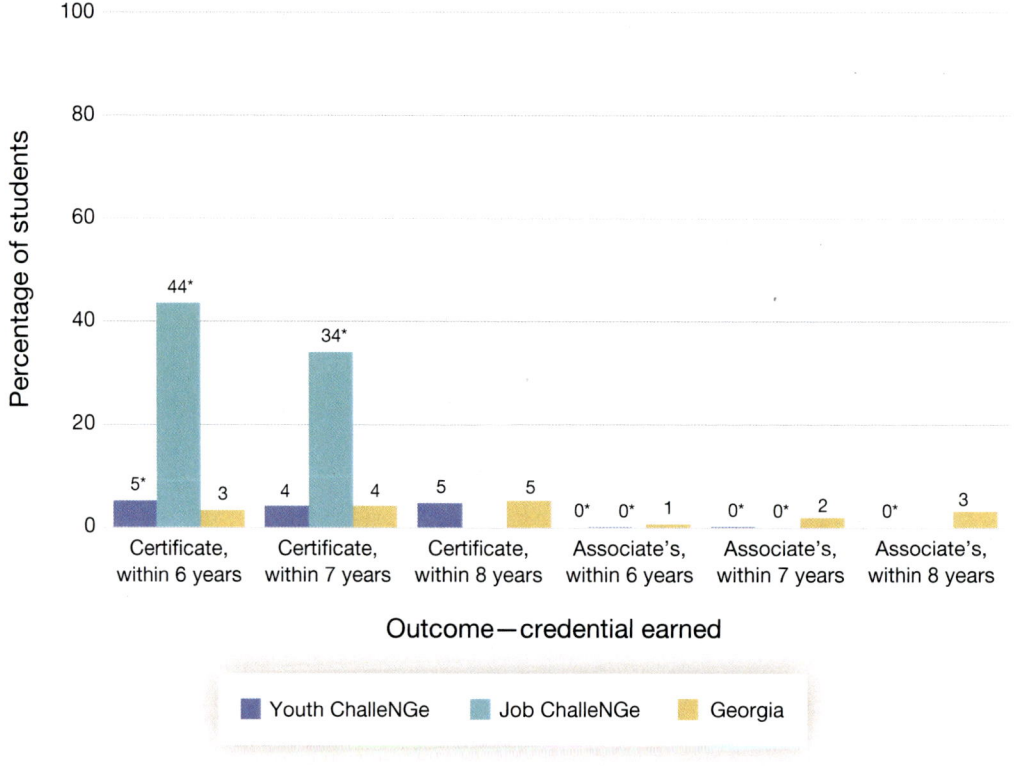

NOTE: *Within x years* refers to the time frame since someone's first 8th-grade attendance in the Georgia public school system. We suppressed the Job ChalleNGe results in the "Certificate, within 8 years" category because of sample size restrictions. Asterisks indicate instances where the difference between the Youth or Job ChalleNGe average characteristic is significantly different from the average characteristic for all public school students in Georgia ($p < 0.05$).

Next we examine the labor force participation in Georgia by age group, presented in Figure 4.6. The labor force participation of Youth and Job ChalleNGe graduates is higher than that of students in the state across all years, and the trend is similar between younger and older students.

FIGURE 4.6

Labor Force Participation of Youth and Job ChalleNGe Graduates Compared with Students in Georgia

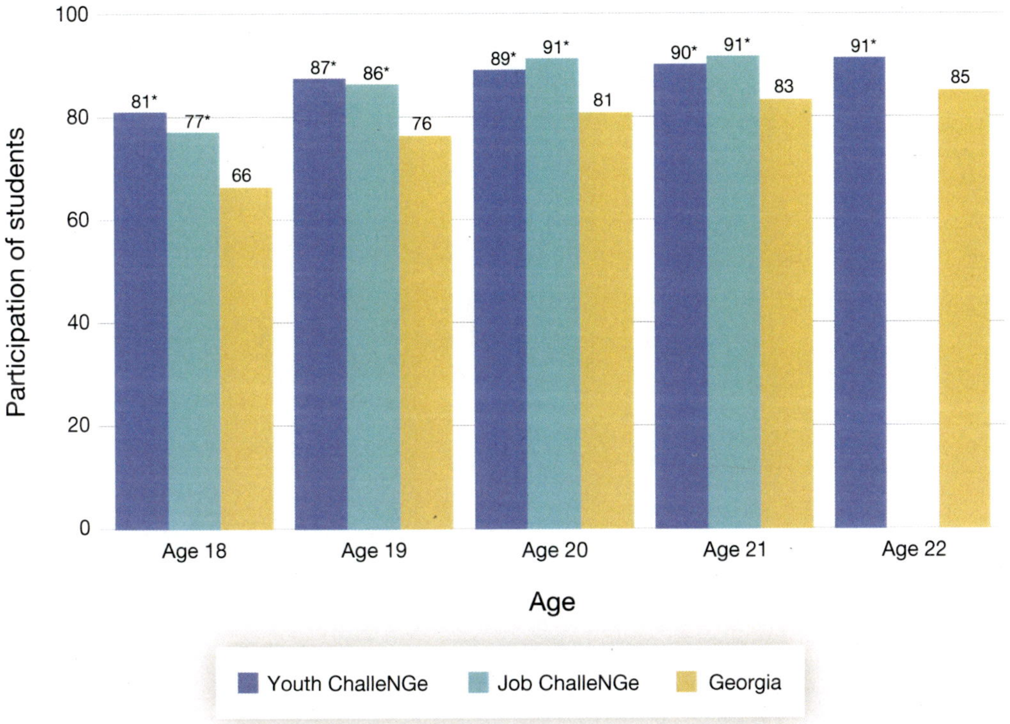

NOTE: We suppressed the Job ChalleNGe results at age 22 due to sample size restrictions. Asterisks indicate instances where the difference between the Youth or Job ChalleNGe average characteristic is significantly different from the average characteristic for all public school students in Georgia ($p < 0.05$).

Figure 4.7 displays the annual wages of Youth and Job ChalleNGe graduates compared with those of all youth in Georgia. In general, while Job ChalleNGe graduates earn more when they are younger, by age 20–21 their earnings fall behind the state average. In the 17–18 age category, average annual wage is $6,343 for Job ChalleNGe participants and $5,657 for youth in Georgia, whereas in the 20–21 age category, average annual wage is $11,664 for Job ChalleNGe participants and $13,794 for youth in Georgia. Annual wage differences between Job ChalleNGe graduates and youth in the state are particularly large. It is important to note that, while the descriptive comparisons are informative, they do not account for differences in youth characteristics, and, therefore, they cannot be considered causal.

What Is the Impact of Youth ChalleNGe on Postsecondary and Labor Force Outcomes?

We find mixed impacts of Youth ChalleNGe on long-term outcomes for youth in Georgia. Focusing first on enrollment in two-year institutions, we do not find a statistically signif-

FIGURE 4.7

Annual Wages of Youth and Job ChalleNGe Graduates Compared with Students in Georgia

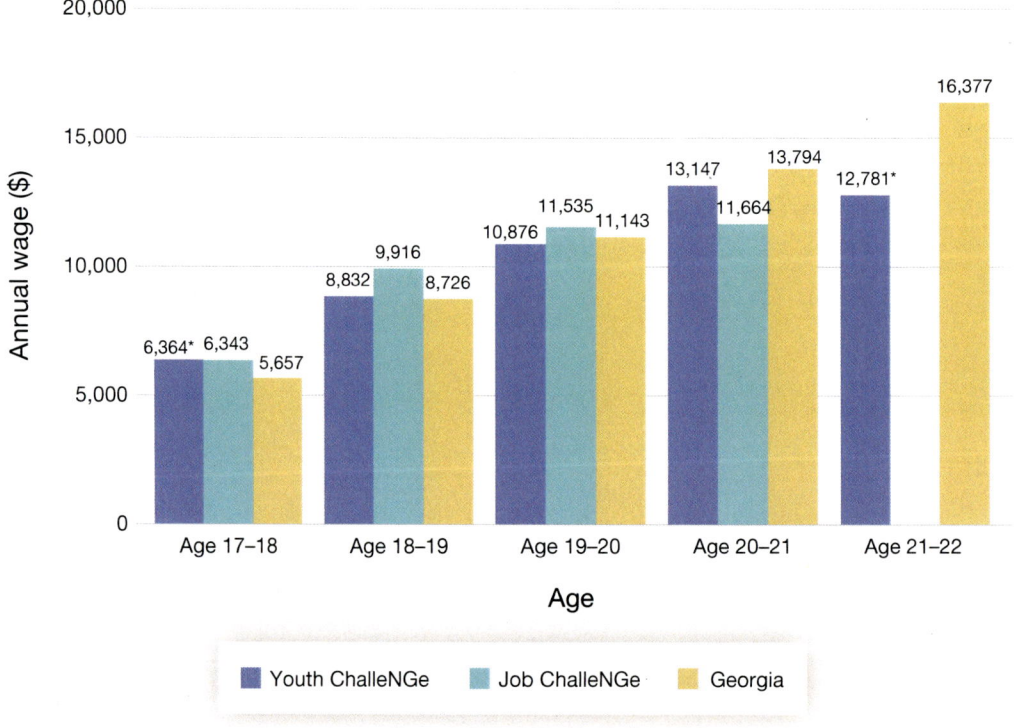

NOTE: We suppressed the Job ChalleNGe results in the age 21–22 category due to sample size restrictions. Asterisks indicate instances where the difference between the Youth or Job ChalleNGe average characteristic is significantly different from the average characteristic for all public school students in Georgia ($p < 0.05$).

icant effect of Youth ChalleNGe on enrollment for any of the time frames examined (see Figure 4.8). Accounting for differences with the comparison group (youth who did not participate in Youth ChalleNGe) by applying the propensity weights results in different estimates here and throughout this section, as opposed to simply comparing means, as we presented in the results for research question 2.[14]

The effect of Youth ChalleNGe on certificate attainment is small and statistically significant (see Figure 4.9). The certificate effect increases as the time frame for the measure expands, going from 4 percentage points to 8 percentage points. The effect of the program on attainment of an associate's degree is not statistically significant. The rates of associate degree

---

[14] The propensity weighting models for each outcome were successful in reducing the difference in the observable characteristics of the treatment and weighted comparison groups. In Appendix B, Figures B.1 through B.11 display the standardized mean differences for each characteristic used in the first-stage weighting models and show how the weighting reduces the standardized difference between the treatment group (Youth ChalleNGe graduates) and the comparison group (non–Youth ChalleNGe graduates).

FIGURE 4.8

Impact of Youth ChalleNGe on Enrollment in a Two-Year Institution

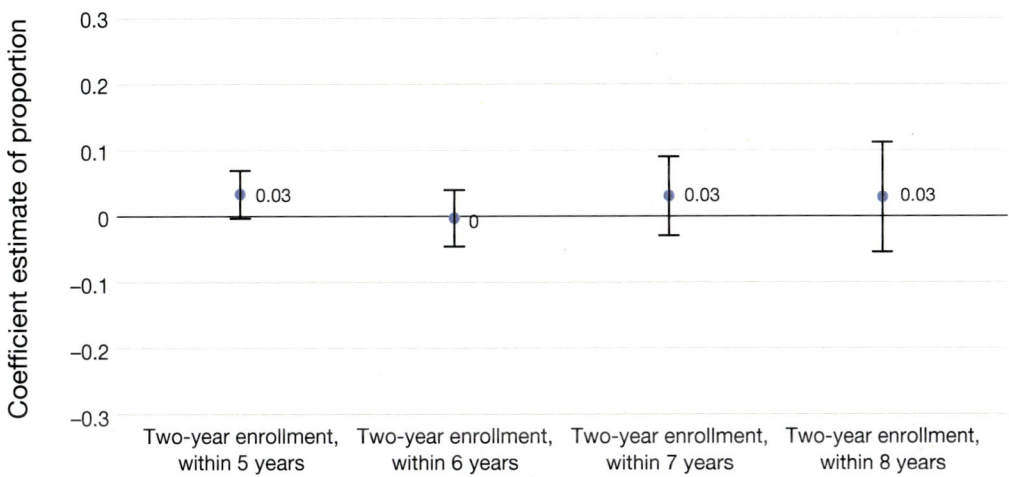

NOTE: The blue dots represent the coefficient estimates from separate regressions, and whiskers display the 95-percent confidence interval around the estimates. When the whiskers do not cross the 0 line, the estimate is statistically significant.

FIGURE 4.9

Impact of Youth ChalleNGe on Postsecondary Credentials

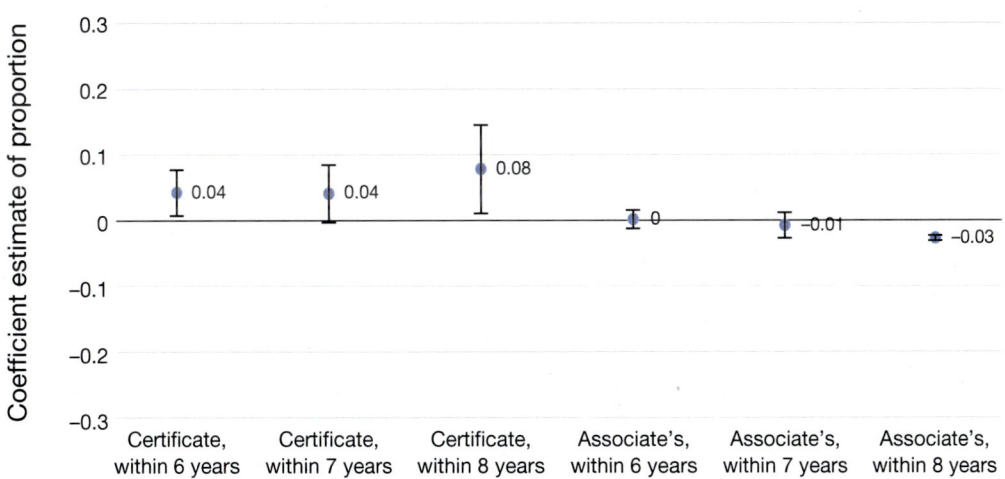

NOTE: The blue dots represent the coefficient estimates from separate regressions, and whiskers display 95-percent confidence intervals around the estimates from the regression models. When the whiskers do not cross the 0 line, the estimate is statistically significant.

attainment are low for the entire sample in the time frame we measure this outcome, and, therefore, we may not have sufficient time to observe youth obtaining this credential.

The program has a positive effect on labor force participation rates, starting at 12 percentage points for people in the 17–18 age range and 6 percentage points for people in the 21–22 age range, compared with those of matched comparison youth—an effect that is statistically significant (see Figure 4.10). This effect is persistent throughout the sample time frame in which we measure this outcome.

When we examine the impact of Youth ChalleNGe on annual wages, we find small effects for youth aged 17–18 through 19–20 (and these effects are not statistically significant in two of the three cases), whereas for youth aged 20–21 and 21–22, we find negative and statistically significant effects (see Figure 4.11). The annual wage effect to youth aged 20–21 is −$2,100, and for youth aged 21–22, it is −$3,900 relative to the matched comparison group.

FIGURE 4.10

Impact of Youth ChalleNGe on Labor Force Participation

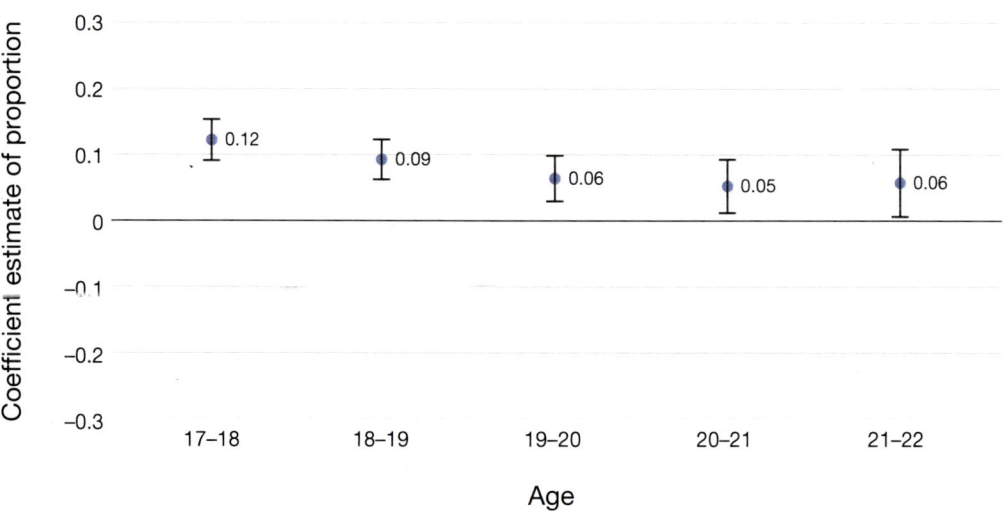

NOTE: The blue dots represent the coefficient estimates from separate regressions, and whiskers display the 95-percent confidence interval around the estimates. When the whiskers do not cross the 0 line, the estimate is statistically significant.

FIGURE 4.11

Impact of Youth ChalleNGe on Annual Wages

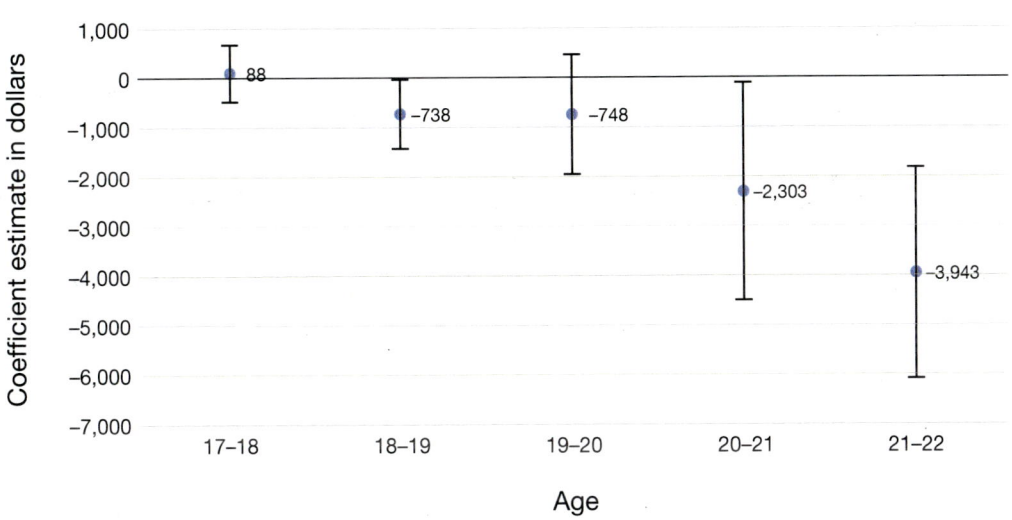

NOTE: The blue dots represent the coefficient estimates from separate regressions, and whiskers display the 95-percent confidence interval around the estimates. When the whiskers do not cross the 0 line, the estimate is statistically significant.

Limitations

Our analysis is the first to use SLDS information on K–12 school, postsecondary, and labor force measures at the individual level to analyze how Youth and Job ChalleNGe graduates compare with youth in the state of Georgia and to estimate the impact of the Youth ChalleNGe program on long-term outcomes. While this is a major advancement from prior work, our analysis does have limitations.

In terms of the data we use, one limitation we face is the length of the panel. We have ten or fewer years of data to track the impact of a program that takes place when students are in grades 9–11, so this does not leave many years to follow students and observe long-term outcomes. A related issue is that we are *not* able to analyze the impact of the program on recent graduates because they have not aged into our analysis sample. If the programs made significant changes recently that affect long-term outcomes, the analysis does not reflect these changes. In addition, our analysis uses data from a single state; therefore, our findings may not generalize to other Youth and Job ChalleNGe programs outside of Georgia.

Another limitation of the data is that by relying on administrative records from GA•AWARDs, our analysis may be biased by missing data. Specifically, because administrative records from this system include only youth who stay in Georgia for postsecondary education and employment, our analysis may be biased by migration of youth out of the state (Foote and Stange, 2022). For example, when we observe zero quarterly wages, we cannot distinguish whether the youth who is absent from state administrative earnings data is truly not working or is working in another state. Prior work has found that migration is higher for those at the top end of the earnings distribution. This may therefore be an issue when comparing Youth and Job ChalleNGe graduates with all students in Georgia. We believe that this issue is less of a concern when comparing Youth and Job ChalleNGe graduates with one another because they are at the lower end of the distribution in state earnings.

In regard to the analytic methods, the propensity score weighting regression approach that we use controls for observable differences in youth characteristics before participation in the program, but we are not able to control for measures that may affect students' outcomes if they are not included in the data. Therefore, there may be unobserved (to the researcher) differences that are not captured in our model between Youth ChalleNGe graduates and comparison youth, which do not allow us to completely account for selection into the program. It is notable that if these unobserved differences are correlated with the observed measures, then our results are less likely to be affected by this issue.

Conclusion

In this chapter, we examined the characteristics and long-term outcomes for Youth and Job ChalleNGe graduates and estimated the impact of the Youth ChalleNGe program on postsecondary enrollment, postsecondary credentialing, labor market participation, and annual wages. We used the Georgia SLDS to conduct this analysis.

We found that the Youth ChalleNGe program draws youth from across the state of Georgia, with more than 50 percent of middle and high schools and more than 70 percent of districts having at least one student enrolled in the program. We also found that Youth and Job ChalleNGe graduates differ from the average student in the state: They are less likely to be female, more likely to be Black, more likely to be economically disadvantaged, and more likely to be SWD compared with all students in Georgia.

Not surprisingly, graduates from Youth and Job ChalleNGe are also more likely to be struggling in 8th grade (before enrolling in the program) than the average student in the state: They are more likely to have unexcused absences; have more disciplinary incidents, such as suspensions in and out of school; and perform significantly worse on standardized tests.

When we compare Job ChalleNGe graduates with Youth ChalleNGe graduates on postsecondary outcomes, we find that Job ChalleNGe graduates have much higher rates of enrollment in two-year postsecondary institutions and earn postsecondary certificates at higher rates than Youth ChalleNGe graduates, with differences around 50 percentage points. Comparing labor market outcomes between the two groups, we find similar labor force participation rates and that younger Youth ChalleNGe graduates have lower annual wages than Job ChalleNGe graduates, but this trend reverses at age 20–21. The combination of these two findings may reflect the fact that youth who graduate Job ChalleNGe are progressing to completing postsecondary credentials and therefore are not working as much as Youth ChalleNGe graduates.

When we compare the postsecondary and labor market outcomes for Youth and Job ChalleNGe graduates with those of the rest of the state, we find that enrollment in two-year institutions and certificate attainment rates are higher for Job ChalleNGe graduates compared with all youth in Georgia. We also find that Youth and Job ChalleNGe graduates are working at higher rates than youth the same age in Georgia.

The differences in outcomes between Youth and Job ChalleNGe graduates are worthy of additional attention. Although Job ChalleNGe participants are a subset of Youth ChalleNGe graduates, the markedly positive outcomes observed among Job ChalleNGe participants could emerge from especially effective aspects of the Job ChalleNGe program, from key differences between Job ChalleNGe and other Youth ChalleNGe participants, or from some combination of the two. First, the combination of Youth and Job ChalleNGe may be sufficient to ensure better outcomes in postsecondary enrollment and certificate completion (in other words, Youth ChalleNGe's five-and-a-half-month length coupled with its broad focus across the core components may be insufficient to prepare many participants for additional success in the postsecondary arena). But Job ChalleNGe participants also may differ from Youth ChalleNGe participants in important ways. The Job ChalleNGe program is a more recent addition to the state's youth programs, so Job ChalleNGe graduates may differ due to long-term trends in the state. Our analytic framework of comparing participants by age should help to correct for this. A more likely source of these differences is that Job ChalleNGe participants may be *positively selected* from other Youth ChalleNGe graduates within any given class or period. The selection could come about in several different ways. Job ChalleNGe participants are willing to be away from home for an additional five-and-a-half months after completing Youth ChalleNGe; this may not be the case for all Youth ChalleNGe graduates. The Job ChalleNGe programs select from applicants during periods of over-subscription, and Job ChalleNGe staff communicate frequently with Youth ChalleNGe staff to identify and attract those Youth ChalleNGe participants who (in the judgment of the staff) will thrive at the Job ChalleNGe program. Additionally, Job ChalleNGe may attract or retain the most academically motivated and talented of the Youth ChalleNGe graduates. We are unable to discern between these potential mechanisms within this current framework, but these are appropriate areas for future analyses.

Finally, we note another limitation created by the data availability. When we estimate the impact of Youth ChalleNGe on long-term outcomes by comparing Youth ChalleNGe graduates and other youth with similar backgrounds, we find mixed results: We find positive and statistically significant effects on attainment of certificates and labor force participation, but no statistically significant effects on enrollment in two-year institutions or associate's degree attainment. In most cases, the differences in earnings are not statistically significant in the time frame that we study. Because of the short timeline in which we are able to track graduates, the real long-term effects of the Youth ChalleNGe program may not yet be apparent. This, too, suggests a need for additional analyses.

CHAPTER 5

Summary and Recommendations

Youth ChalleNGe has graduated nearly 200,000 young people since its inception in 1993 (Wenger, Cottrell, and Wrabel, 2023). The Job ChalleNGe program builds on the supports provided to Youth ChalleNGe graduates, expanding access to job training and education credentialing opportunities. RAND researchers have been conducting research on these programs since 2016 and have amassed data and insights about program operations, challenges, and successes. Most of our prior research relied on information provided by ChalleNGe staff through cadet data files, interviews, and site visits. In this report, we expand on our previous work by integrating the perspective of Job ChalleNGe participants and leveraging external statewide education and labor administrative data. These analyses provide new insights for ChalleNGe leadership and individual sites to use in their decisionmaking.

The analyses we present in this project capstone report were guided by key research tasks:

- Collect detailed data on Youth ChalleNGe site and produce an annual report.
- Design and conduct an implementation and outcomes study of Job ChalleNGe.
- Conduct small pilot projects occurring within one or more program sites.

To complete these tasks, we gathered annual data on Youth ChalleNGe sites and participants, collected data and conducted analyses necessary to complete an implementation and outcomes study of Job ChalleNGe, and procured external administrative data to analyze longer-term program outcomes. This report builds on RAND's prior ChalleNGe research by examining the program's alignment with mission to serve at-risk youth, identifying trends in participation using data beyond those provided by ChalleNGe sites, identifying available approaches to measure longer-term outcomes and assess those approaches, and providing program leadership at DoD, the National Guard Bureau, and the sites with a deeper understanding of program implementation and outcomes.

We began this report by describing longitudinal trends in Youth ChalleNGe program participation and program completion. We also present a series of analyses on the communities and circumstances from which cadets are drawn. Chapter 2 demonstrates the alignment between the program's mission and the population served. Chapters 3 and 4 describe our implementation and outcome studies. Chapter 3 provides findings related to Job ChalleNGe implementation, including perspectives of both staff and participants. Chapter 4 describes our analysis of the post-program outcomes—namely, educational attainment and labor market participation—of Youth and Job ChalleNGe participants using state administrative data from Georgia. In what follows, we draw across the analyses presented throughout this report to provide a summary of key findings.

Summary of Key Findings

Youth ChalleNGe and Job ChalleNGe both seek to provide opportunities for young people at risk of not earning a high school diploma to develop academic, life, career, and leadership skills. Youth ChalleNGe typically serves more than 10,000 young people each year. The programs are designed to serve individuals who struggle in school, many of whom would be expected to come from lower-income families. Using both national and state data, we find that Youth and Job ChalleNGe are meeting this aspect of their missions by serving young people from under-resourced and historically disadvantaged communities; we find that most cadets come from less-advantaged communities. This result is driven by cadets from historically marginalized backgrounds, who make up the majority of Youth ChalleNGe participants. Black and Latino cadets, for example, are more likely to come from communities with increased levels of disadvantage as compared with their White counterparts and to the broader U.S. population. Given the communities from which participants are drawn, program graduates are likely to return to communities with below-average resources and weaker-than-average social networks, which has implications for participants' post-program placement prospects.

One opportunity for graduates to receive additional supports in the Youth ChalleNGe post-residential phase, especially for job skills and education credentials, is the Job ChalleNGe program. Our analyses of six program sites suggest that Job ChalleNGe staff are committed to providing educational and job training opportunities to participants and ensuring that participants find productive opportunities following program completion. Staff indicate that a wide array of resources, supports, and services is made available to Job ChalleNGe participants to enhance their development of knowledge, skills, and abilities beyond those provided in the job training programs. But sites predominantly rely on ChalleNGe-provided resources and staff and less commonly utilize their educational or training partner resources and staff in the provision of these supports.

One limitation we identified in the offering of these supports and services is the current staffing levels of Job ChalleNGe. We heard from both participants and staff at the sites that hiring staff and current staff shortages were areas of concern. These difficulties are not unique to Job ChalleNGe; our prior analyses have identified similar difficulties for Youth ChalleNGe sites (see Wenger et al., 2024; Wenger, Cottrell, and Wrabel, 2023). What is novel in this case, however, is the participant perspective on how this issue directly shapes and influences their experience in the program. Participants expressed that staffing shortages often limited academic and social opportunities available to them. That said, Job ChalleNGe provides opportunities that participants suggest they would not have or would be less likely to take up without support of the program. Finally, most participants wish the length of the program, however, was better aligned with the amount of time needed to complete meaningful job certifications.

Participants also reported misalignment between how the Job ChalleNGe program is advertised to them prior to participation and the lived experience when in the program; this misalignment has led to dissatisfaction or frustration while they are in the program. These feelings were also shaped by the residential nature of the program, experiencing homesickness, limited opportunities to visit or communicate with family members, and worries about securing employment after being away from home and prior jobs for extended periods.

We were able to leverage data from Georgia as a proof-of-concept measurement of long-term outcomes for Youth and Job ChalleNGe program graduates. While this analysis was not without limitations, such as having a relatively short time frame of data to observe and measure outcomes and difficulties in identifying appropriate comparison groups for Youth and Job ChalleNGe graduates, these analyses do provide preliminary insights of program effects, at least in one state. We find that attending Youth ChalleNGe did not affect the rate of postsecondary enrollment, but it did have a positive effect on completion of postsecondary credentials; moreover, the effect increased in magnitude over time. This suggests that Youth ChalleNGe may help graduates develop skills and competencies (e.g., self-efficacy, persistence in the face of difficulty) that enhance their ability to handle the challenges of postsecondary education. We also found that Youth ChalleNGe had a positive effect on labor force participation, although we only found a small positive effect on annual wages for younger participants and negative effects for older participants. It is important to note, however, that we cannot determine whether Youth ChalleNGe participants realized lower annual wages than comparative peers because they were differentially enrolled in education and training programs while working, they worked fewer hours, or they worked different types of jobs. Finally, while we could not estimate the causal impact of Job ChalleNGe, we do see descriptive trends that Job ChalleNGe participants had higher rates of postsecondary enrollment, credential earning, and labor force participation than non-ChalleNGe students in Georgia. Analyses using additional years of data, including information on hours worked, job titles, and industry and occupation, could help address these limitations. Next, we present a set of recommendations drawn from the results of the analyses we performed, and we conclude with opportunities for future research.

Recommendations

Identify Opportunities to Assist Graduates Who May Require Additional Supports to Realize the Benefits of the Program

The long-term success of Youth and Job ChalleNGe is heavily dependent on graduates' actions once they enter the post-residential phase of the program. Most of these individuals return home to the communities in which they lived prior to enrolling in the ChalleNGe program, and they seek educational and employment opportunities in those communities. As our analyses suggest, the communities these individuals come from have, on average, lower levels of education and youth labor force participation, lower household income, and lower rates of economic connectedness. Cadets from historically marginalized racial and ethnic groups come from communities that are more disadvantaged than those of their White peers. This suggests that these communities may not provide sufficient educational or labor market opportunities that will help launch graduates onto a successful trajectory. Therefore, program graduates may need assistance identifying and navigating productive post-residential opportunities. As the program is currently designed, cadet mentors provide most of the cadet support during this period of the program, but ChalleNGe may need to consider how it structures and resources the post-residential phase to ensure that graduates leverage their program experience for positive long-term benefit. We suspect that program staff are well aware of these issues; indeed, they may have developed specific strategies to provide additional support. Information-sharing, as well as test cases or pilot projects, may help sites identify feasible strategies to better assist cadets.

Utilize the Full Scope of Resources Provided by Job ChalleNGe Training and Education Partners

Resource constraints, particularly in staffing, were identified by both Job ChalleNGe staff and participants. Most Job ChalleNGe staff also reported that they had not connected participants with supports provided by community college partners. Job ChalleNGe is paying for these resources, through participation tuition, and it appears that these resources are not fully leveraged to benefit participants. Such services may even help alleviate the specific pressures on Job ChalleNGe to offer comprehensive physical and mental health services. Supports may also be available to identify potential employers, trade schools to which students can transfer courses and credits, and other post-residential opportunities for Job ChalleNGe graduates. Where educators and training partners have connections with industry partners and employers, they should seek opportunities to leverage these relationships to better position participants for success. Some sites have already begun using instructors to provide such connections, and lessons may provide examples that other sites can follow.

Support Job ChalleNGe Sites to Develop Consistent Messaging and Recruitment Materials

As Youth ChalleNGe cadets prepare for the post-residential phase, many of the individuals in states offering a Job ChalleNGe program will be interested to learn about the benefits of the program, how the program is similar to or different from Youth ChalleNGe, and whether the offered training programs and resulting credentials align with their own interests. Now that the effects of the pandemic have largely receded and sites have returned to more normal operations, sites must ensure that the experience conveyed to interested cadets accurately represents the lived experiences of the individuals who have participated in the program.

Sites should communicate clearly about what credentials and certifications students may or may not earn during the program, what to expect for living and meal arrangements, and how time is structured and the extent to which participants should expect more flexibility or freedom than what Youth ChalleNGe permits.

Our analyses suggest that current messaging about what the program offers or how the program operates is not sufficiently aligned with participants' experiences. Sites may consider asking Job ChalleNGe participants to speak honestly with interested Youth ChalleNGe cadets to provide a first-person account of the program. Providing consistent messaging helps establish accurate expectations for future Job ChalleNGe participants and may generate additional program satisfaction among participants. Developing materials that can be easily shared to support such conversations may also support engagements with potential employers, local organizations, and potential training or education partners.

Continue Exploring Avenues for Data Collection and Long-Term Outcome Analyses

Our team has explored various ways of collecting and assessing the long-term outcomes of program participants. In Wenger, Wrabel, and colleagues (2022), we specifically named three approaches: maintain contact with each graduate, periodically survey graduates, or match graduates to state or national existing data systems. The goal of any such effort is to understand how well the program is producing the intended outcomes. These insights will help identify aspects of the programs that may benefit from additional capacity-building and support, which should lead to improved outcomes for graduates of Youth and Job ChalleNGe in the years that follow.

In Chapter 4, we presented analyses of matching cadets with available external state-level data sources. A benefit of such an approach is access to comprehensive data on the population of ChalleNGe graduates who remain within the state. This approach comes with its own challenges and burdens, including the amount of time and administrative processes necessary to obtain data permissions and subsequent data, a substantive lag in when data become available, and the length of a data panel needed to amass a sufficient sample and observe outcomes. A particular concern is that too few years of data could lead to inaccurate conclusions of no or negative program effects when, in fact, there was insufficient time to observe the outcome in the data. Moreover, given the operations of ChalleNGe across multiple states, there is a very high cost in establishing data use agreements with each participating state to fully assess the long-term outcomes of program participation. Some states are developing strategies to produce specialized reports from their SLDS for programs within their state; this strategy is promising, as it would require far fewer program resources. But as of this writing, the details of these programs and the resources required remain unclear.

The third option for measuring outcomes is linking ChalleNGe data with existing national datasets and using external (centrally administered) surveys, including a complete sampling and a strategic or representative sampling, of graduates. Survey data may provide nuance and perceptions from graduates that administrative data are unable to capture (e.g., quality of and satisfaction with life); national administrative data have the benefit of comprehensive information on program graduates regardless of whether they have moved since program participation. These approaches each require access to a substantial amount of personally identifiable information on cadets (or their family members if the cadet is younger than age 18). RAND currently is working in this area and will continue to advance data collection efforts to provide DoD with additional insights on how to best measure long-term outcomes of the Youth and Job ChalleNGe programs.

Areas for Future Research

Over the course of two projects, the RAND team has systematically defined and explored options for collecting and assessing data and information on ChalleNGe participants' long-term outcomes. As described in the first project's capstone report, the primary approaches RAND identified include maintaining contact with each graduate, periodically surveying graduates, and matching graduates to state or national existing data systems (more details available in Wenger, Wrabel, et al., 2022). Our efforts to date on these approaches have identified additional areas of analysis that would further support ChalleNGe in measuring the long-term outcomes produced by the programs.

Working with a single site several years ago, we assisted in the development of a survey of graduates (again, see Wenger, Wrabel, et al., 2022). This effort was successful, albeit with substantial effort on the part of program staff. As part of the current project, we attempted to survey Job ChalleNGe participants during their residential phase and Job ChalleNGe graduates (see Appendix C for a description of these efforts). We found that this approach did not rise to the response level necessary for high-quality analysis or a fair determination of program performance. In both instances, the burden on site-level staff for implementing these data collection efforts was substantive and prohibitive. Future research on ChalleNGe should implement practices to maintain contact with graduates and periodically survey graduates that remove or significantly reduce the burden from individual site staff. Such practices could include leveraging a ChalleNGe-wide database to centralize outreach and communication and relying on external entities to implement these efforts on behalf of ChalleNGe.

Our analyses using the Georgia SLDS demonstrate that even administrative data are not without limitations and potential areas for improvement. Analyses should also be expanded to multiple states or to leverage federally available data to (1) determine whether Georgia's ChalleNGe trends are consistent with those of other programs, (2) understand the extent to which program graduates travel across state lines and cannot be observed in a single-state data system, (3) estimate impacts programwide rather than at the site or state level, and (4) generate a sufficient sample of Job ChalleNGe participants to estimate causal impacts of attending the program. We would recommend, where available, examining rates of high-school credential earning (e.g., traditional diploma, GED), as well as postsecondary credits and credentials earned and the rate of transfer between two-year and four-year postsecondary institutions; these measures represent educational achievements after program participation. We would also suggest expanding on the labor market data analyzed to include the number and types of jobs a person works, the benefits available through the job, and the hourly pay rate rather than overall earnings; these data points may provide important context for the identified trends. Collecting data on other aspects of graduates' lives, such as family formation, civic engagement, or overall health, could provide information about other impacts of ChalleNGe outside of the academic and labor market arenas.

Finally, we recommend the continued analyses of program trends to support the program and help build capacity nationally and locally to best serve participants and graduates. One such extension of prior work is additional examination of staff across sites. To date, only counts of staff members have been analyzed; expanding the staff analyses to be conducted at the person level within sites rather than at the site level, and to include such information as demographics and years of experience, may provide additional insights into mechanisms that influence program operations and outcomes. Such analyses could support both Youth ChalleNGe and Job ChalleNGe, especially as the programs expand into new states and seek to serve larger numbers of young people each year.

Additional Information About Neighborhood Analyses

Additional Information on Data and Methods

Data used for this analysis came from three different sources: administrative data for all Youth ChalleNGe cadets from 2016 through 2021 (collected by the RAND team), Opportunity Insights social capital data, and zip code–level ACS data. Youth ChalleNGe data included information on race and ethnicity, gender, the Youth ChalleNGe program site, year, and class, and each cadet's home zip code.[1] The total sample of Youth ChalleNGe cadets was 68,198 with relatively even distribution across years, although Youth ChalleNGe attendance did decline from 2020 onward.

The Opportunity Insights social capital data contained zip code–level information on economic connectedness for most zip codes (23,028 in total) in the 50 U.S. states and Washington, D.C., using data collected from Facebook users. The main period of the study was 2018, so all variables capture a static glance at economic connections across zip codes for that period. Our analysis focuses on four main variables:

- *Economic connectedness* measures the share of high-SES friends among low-SES individuals averaged among all the low-SES individuals within a zip code.
- *Clustering* measures the average fraction of an individual's friend pairs who are also friends with each other.
- *Volunteering rate* calculates the percentage of Facebook users who are members of a group predicted to be about volunteering or activism based on the group's title and characteristics.
- *Civic organizations* counts the number of Facebook pages predicted to be public-good pages per 1,000 users in the zip code. This is based on page title, category, and other characteristics.

---

[1] RAND's Youth ChalleNGe cadet data begin in 2015; however, we do not have zip codes for the cadets in 2015, so we dropped that year of data from these analyses.

ACS variables are also captured at the zip code level for a static period in time. In this case, they represent a five-year average from 2016 through 2020. Data exist for 32,989 zip codes and, like the social capital data, represent most zip codes in the 50 states and Washington, D.C. The variables examined from this data include demographics on the percentage of the zip code population who are White, foreign born, and have less than a high school education. We also looked at several measures of financial well-being and labor force participation. We used median household income, household poverty, child poverty (measured as the percentage of households with children aged 5–17 with income below the poverty line), household crowding (we use the U.S. Census Bureau definition of a crowded household, which is one with more than one person per bedroom), as well as overall and youth labor force participation, unemployment rates, and youth unemployment (for those aged 16–23).

Data were merged by zip code for each data source, resulting in slightly different numbers of observations depending on the data source. We initially cleaned and dropped missing zip codes from the Youth ChalleNGe data. About 1 percent of the original sample of 68,198 cadets could not be matched due to missing or nonstandard zip codes; after this, the analytic file included 67,573 cadets from 10,371 distinct zip codes. About 5 percent of the cadets could not be matched to the ACS data; about 8 percent could not be matched to the social capital data. Neither the social capital nor ACS data provided any data for Puerto Rico zip codes; therefore, cadets from the Puerto Rico site could not be matched to community measures and are not included in any of the following analyses. Otherwise, there are some unmatched cadets from zip codes where data are masked in the social capital or ACS sources due to limited sample sizes. When merging to the social capital data, we are left with a sample of 62,316 cadets. For the ACS data, the sample is 64,300 cadets.

To conduct the analysis, we calculated mean estimates for Youth ChalleNGe cadets, which were then compared with population-weighted means for all zip codes.[2] Among the Youth ChalleNGe cadets, we also examined differences in subgroups by race and ethnicity (White and non-White averages) and gender (male and female averages). We determined statistical significance between groups based on two-way t-tests. We also calculated overall descriptive statistics classifying each zip code in the social capital and ACS data as a Youth ChalleNGe or non–Youth ChalleNGe zip code. A zip code was included in the Youth ChalleNGe group if at least one cadet was recruited from that zip code in the period in question. All other zip codes were coded as non–Youth ChalleNGe. Adjusted Wald tests were used to flag where the overall mean values varied between Youth ChalleNGe and non–Youth ChalleNGe zip codes.

We further tested and substantiated the mean differences that we found through OLS regression analyses for each variable; models included measures of cadet race and ethnicity and gender, as well as year and U.S. Census division. We also tested the sample using two-way fixed effects models with a time trend and site-level fixed effects. This allowed us to deter-

---

[2] In Chapter 4, we use the word *community* to describe the unit of analysis, but we also note that analyses are actually carried out at the zip code level. Throughout this appendix, we use the more precise and technical term *zip code*.

mine whether any time trends and racial or gender differences that we observed in the outcome variables were driven primarily by differences across sites or whether there were also differences that occurred between those subgroups and over time within each of the sites. In addition to these regression checks, we used robustness checks applied to different samples and periods. These are described in greater detail in a subsequent section.

Results for All Variables Comparing Zip Codes with Cadets to All U.S. Zip Codes

A full reporting of all the variables that we examined for the Youth ChalleNGe cadets are included in Table A.1. These compare mean values for the zip codes of all Youth ChalleNGe cadets weighted by the number of cadets from each zip code to a benchmark of population-

TABLE A.1

Economic and Social Measures: Youth ChalleNGe Cadets Versus Benchmark U.S. Zip Codes

Zip Code–Level Variable	Youth ChalleNGe Cadets' Zip Codes	All U.S. Zip Codes (Weighted by Population)
Economic connectedness	0.786 (0.194)	0.869 (0.229)
Clustering	0.099 (0.020)	0.095 (0.016)
Volunteer rates	0.064 (0.031)	0.066 (0.030)
Civic organizations	0.013 (0.013)	0.015 (0.020)
Percentage White	0.624 (0.262)	0.704 (0.222)
Percentage foreign born	0.096 (0.106)	0.135 (0.127)
Percentage with less than high school education	0.134 (0.085)	0.117 (0.087)
Percentage living in crowded households	0.040 (0.051)	0.036 (0.043)
Median income ($)	60,670 (21,568)	70,753 (28,795)
Household poverty rate	0.149 (0.082)	0.126 (0.078)
Child poverty rate	0.183 (0.121)	0.146 (0.110)
Percentage using public assistance	0.028 (0.025)	0.025 (0.021)
Labor force participation	0.618 (0.082)	0.635 (0.082)
Youth labor force participation	0.581 (0.114)	0.593 (0.114)
Unemployment rate	0.063 (0.037)	0.055 (0.029)
Youth unemployment rate	0.135 (0.093)	0.118 (0.078)

SOURCES: Authors' calculations from RAND annual collections, Youth ChalleNGe classes including 2016–2021; ACS five-year averages, 2016–2020 (U.S. Census Bureau, 2022); and Opportunity Insights data (Opportunity Insights, undated). These sources are described in more detail at the beginning of this appendix. Standard errors are included in parentheses.

weighted mean values for all U.S. zip codes. Standard errors are also noted. In general, across all of the measures, Youth ChalleNGe cadets come from zip codes that are less economically connected, more disadvantaged, and more diverse than the average U.S. zip code. A selection of these means is reported in Chapter 2, Figure 2.1, to highlight the most notable and statistically significant differences.

We repeated the same analysis, now comparing Youth ChalleNGe and non–Youth ChalleNGe zip codes (see Table A.2).[3] Just 39 percent of the Opportunity Insights zip codes and 30 percent of the ACS zip codes had sent any participants to the Youth ChalleNGe program, indicating strong clustering in the areas that cadets are drawn from.

In this case, both means and standard deviations are reported and weighted by zip code population rather than by the number of cadets coming from a specific zip code. The general trend in the variables is the same as when looking at cadets versus the U.S. average, but now the Youth ChalleNGe zip codes appear slightly less economically disadvantaged than before for most variables. For example, economic connectedness, median household income, and youth labor force participation are now slightly larger but still statistically lower than the non–Youth ChalleNGe zip codes. This suggests that less-advantaged zip codes send more cadets to Youth ChalleNGe.

Differences in Social Capital

The social capital variables captured in the Opportunity Insights data measure the level of connectedness between low-SES and high-SES individuals within a zip code, along with rates of clustering among friends, volunteering rates, and the number of civic organizations. Overall, Youth ChalleNGe cadets come from zip codes that are less economically connected than the average U.S. zip code or than non–Youth ChalleNGe zip codes. The average Youth ChalleNGe cadet comes from a community with levels of economic connectedness of 39 percent compared with the U.S. average of 43 percent. Significant but smaller differences in volunteering rates and civic organizations were observed as well.

---

[3] Every zip code in both the Opportunity Insights and ACS datasets was coded as either one or zero depending on whether it had sent at least one participant to the Youth ChalleNGe program at any point in the sample period.

TABLE A.2

Economic and Social Measures: Mean Differences Between Youth ChalleNGe and Non–Youth ChalleNGe Zip Codes

Zip Code–Level Variable	Youth ChalleNGe Zip Codes (N = 8,938 in Social Capital Data; N = 9,807 in ACS Data)	Non–Youth ChalleNGe Zip Codes (N = 14,090 in Social Capital Data; N = 23,182 in ACS Data)
Economic connectedness	0.830 (0.217)*	0.924 (0.235)
Clustering	0.092 (0.016)*	0.098 (0.016)
Volunteer rates	0.062 (0.030)*	0.071 (0.029)
Civic organizations	0.013 (0.013)*	0.017 (0.026)
Percentage White	0.648 (0.228)*	0.781 (0.187)
Percentage foreign born	0.151 (0.132)*	0.114 (0.118)
Percentage with less than high school education	0.129 (0.090)*	0.101 (0.079)
Percentage living in crowded households	0.043 (0.048)*	0.027 (0.034)
Median income ($)	68,822 (26,341)*	73,431 (31,693)
Household poverty rate	0.131 (0.076)*	0.119 (0.080)
Child poverty rate	0.155 (0.107)*	0.133 (0.114)
Percentage using public assistance	0.026 (0.021)*	0.023 (0.022)
Labor force participation	0.639 (0.073)*	0.630 (0.093)
Youth labor force participation	0.585 (0.099)*	0.605 (0.131)
Unemployment rate	0.058 (0.028)*	0.051 (0.031)
Youth unemployment rate	0.124 (0.072)*	0.109 (0.085)

SOURCES: Authors' calculations from RAND annual collections, Youth ChalleNGe classes including 2016–2021; ACS five-year averages, 2016–2020 (U.S. Census Bureau, 2022); and Opportunity Insights data (Opportunity Insights, undated). These sources are described in more detail at the beginning of this appendix.

NOTE: Standard errors are included in parentheses. Asterisks denote significant differences, at the 5-percent level, between group averages.

There is not strong evidence that cadet social capital background varies substantially based on gender (see Table A.3). However, there is strong evidence that non-White cadets come from zip codes that tend to be substantially less economically connected than the zip codes that White cadets come from. Non-White cadets come from zip codes with an average economic connectedness of 38 percent relative to 41 percent for White cadets. Our regression analyses confirm these differences, and the results appear to be at least partly explained by existing inequalities and segregation in the United States, as Southern and Midwestern divisions had larger disparities in economic connectedness than other areas. Nonetheless, the pattern still existed within sites (after controlling for site-level fixed effects), suggest-

TABLE A.3

Differences in Youth ChalleNGe Cadet Social Capital Outcomes, by Race and Ethnicity and Gender

Zip Code–Level Variable	Male Cadets' Zip Codes	Female Cadets' Zip Codes	White Cadets' Zip Codes	Non-White Cadets' Zip Codes	All U.S. Zip Codes (Weighted by Population)
Economic connectedness	0.786 (0.193)	0.785 (0.195)	0.826 (0.171)*	0.757 (0.204)	0.869 (0.229)
Clustering	0.010 (0.020)*	0.098 (0.019)	0.104 (0.018)*	0.096 (0.020)	0.095 (0.016)
Volunteer rates	0.064 (0.031)	0.064 (0.031)	0.075 (0.031)*	0.056 (0.029)	0.066 (0.030)
Civic organizations	0.013 (0.012)	0.013 (0.014)	0.014 (0.010)	0.013 (0.014)	0.015 (0.020)

SOURCES: Authors' calculations from RAND annual collections, Youth ChalleNGe classes including 2016–2021, and from Opportunity Insights data (Opportunity Insights, undated). These sources are described in more detail at the beginning of this appendix.

NOTE: Asterisks denote significant differences, at the 5-percent level, between group averages by race and ethnicity or gender.

ing that differences by race and ethnicity are a pattern that we would expect to be found at every site as opposed to being primarily explained by differences between the various Youth ChalleNGe sites.

We do not find substantial evidence of changes over time for any of the social capital variables. Recall that the social capital variables were measured at a single point in time; therefore, any changes that we observed would indicate a shift in the types of neighborhoods that produced cadets over time. While there are small positive trends that are statistically significant in the regression results, the magnitudes of the changes are not substantial, indicating a less than 1 percentage point shift in connectedness, volunteering, clustering, and the number of civic organizations. This suggests that, over the time examined, the Youth ChalleNGe program served cadets from neighborhoods with similar levels of social capital. Of course, overall levels of social capital could have changed over this period in a way that is not captured by our data. But given the high levels of correlation between measures of social capital and economic measures, this appears unlikely. The substantial differences that we see are, as noted earlier, between cadets of differing race or ethnicity.

Differences in Demographic Measures

Youth ChalleNGe cadets are more likely to come from zip codes that are less White, have a larger proportion of immigrants, have higher rates of crowding, and are less educated than non–Youth ChalleNGe and the average zip codes. This lends evidence to the notion that Youth ChalleNGe cadets tend to come from more-diverse areas. We summarize this evidence in Table A.4.

There is evidence that female cadets come from more-diverse zip codes with lower education levels, on average, although the magnitude of these differences is generally quite small, less than 1 percent. Among non-White cadets, these differences are far starker. Compared with White

TABLE A.4

Differences in Youth ChalleNGe Cadet Demographics, by Race and Ethnicity and Gender

Zip Code–Level Variable	Male Cadets' Zip Codes	Female Cadets' Zip Codes	White Cadets' Zip Codes	Non-White Cadets' Zip Codes	All U.S. Zip Codes (Weighted by Population)
Percentage White	0.629 (0.262)*	0.606 (0.262)	0.777 (0.182)*	0.509 (0.254)	0.704 (0.222)
Percentage foreign-born	0.092 (0.104)*	0.108 (0.113)	0.053 (0.065)*	0.128 (0.119)	0.135 (0.127)
Percentage with less than a high school education	0.132 (0.084)*	0.139 (0.091)	0.118 (0.069)*	0.146 (0.094)	0.118 (0.087)
Percentage living in crowded households	0.038 (0.049)*	0.046 (0.058)	0.025 (0.026)*	0.051 (0.062)	0.036 (0.043)

SOURCES: Authors' calculations from RAND annual collections, Youth ChalleNGe classes including 2016–2021, and ACS five-year averages, 2016–2020 (U.S. Census Bureau, 2022). These sources are described in more detail at the beginning of this appendix.

NOTE: Asterisks denote significant differences, at the 5-percent level, between group averages by race and ethnicity or gender.

cadets, non-White cadets come from zip codes that are 27 percentage points less White and 8 percentage points more foreign-born, on average. While there are differences across census divisions, these trends exist both across and within sites, indicating that the differences are not being driven by specific sites drawing different cadets but that non-White cadets within each site have substantially different neighborhood backgrounds than their White counterparts.

There is minor evidence that the percentage of foreign-born individuals and the percentage with less than a high school degree by race and ethnicity and gender have decreased slightly over time, with the effect being driven primarily by changes among non-White cadet cohorts since 2020. Nonetheless, these changes are small overall and do not substantially change the pattern observed between White and non-White cadets in terms of the demographic background of the neighborhoods that they come from.

Differences in Poverty and Income Levels

Overall, the neighborhoods that Youth ChalleNGe cadets come from have lower incomes than the average U.S. zip code and the average non–Youth ChalleNGe zip code. The average median household income in a Youth ChalleNGe zip code is $10,000 less than the U.S. population-weighted average, and poverty rates are 2 or more percentage points higher. A detailed understanding of cadets' varied backgrounds may help program staff better tailor programming and reentry advice to the problems that may emerge as cadets reenter their home communities.

There are no substantial differences in median income for cadets' zip code by race and ethnicity or gender. However, non-White cadets come from backgrounds with significantly higher rates of household and child poverty. We present supporting evidence in Table A.5. The zip codes that female and non-White cadets come from also have higher levels of public assistance use on average. These differences remain statistically significant in our regression analyses, indicating that the differences are driven by differences within sites and not just by regional or site-level differences, although those also exist.

The starkest changes in the composition of Youth ChalleNGe cadets over time are in the poverty rates of neighborhoods that Youth ChalleNGe cadets are coming from. These rates capture the average in each zip code from 2016 and 2020. Therefore, the changes in the average observed here do not reflect changes in the poverty rates of specific places over time, but changes in the places that cadets are recruited from over time. After 2018 and continuing to the present, cadets have been recruited from zip codes with lower household and child poverty rates. This change is driven primarily by the recruitment of non-White cadets from zip codes with lower household poverty rates. This shift may make it more challenging for the Youth ChalleNGe program to meet its mission if it is having greater difficulty recruiting cadets from the poorest neighborhoods.

TABLE A.5

Differences in Youth ChalleNGe Cadet Poverty and Income, by Race and Ethnicity and Gender

Zip Code–Level Variable	Male Cadets' Zip Codes	Female Cadets' Zip Codes	White Cadets' Zip Codes	Non-White Cadets' Zip Codes	All U.S. Zip Codes (Weighted by Population)
Median income ($)	60,623 (21,699)	60,823 (21,128)	60,294 (20,188)*	60,949 (22,535)	70,753 (28,795)
Household poverty rate	0.149 (0.082)	0.150 (0.082)	0.139 (0.076)*	0.157 (0.085)	0.126 (0.078)
Child poverty rate	0.183 (0.121)	0.185 (0.118)	0.166 (0.116)*	0.196 (0.122)	0.146 (0.110)
Percentage using public assistance	0.027 (0.025)*	0.030 (0.027)	0.023 (0.022)*	0.031 (0.027)	0.025 (0.021)

SOURCES: Authors' calculations from RAND annual collections, Youth ChalleNGe classes including 2016–2021, and ACS five-year averages, 2016–2020 (U.S. Census Bureau, 2022).

NOTE: Asterisks denote significant differences, at the 5-percent level, between group averages by race and ethnicity or gender.

Differences in Labor Market Outcomes

The final set of variables we examined from the ACS concerned full and youth labor force participation and unemployment. For this analysis, youth were defined as being aged 16–24. Overall, Youth ChalleNGe cadets come from zip codes with higher unemployment rates and lower labor force participation than the U.S. average. The Youth ChalleNGe program should consider how these environments may complicate cadets' future economic mobility and what resources they can provide to support them.

No substantial differences were observed on these variables between male and female cadets. However, non-White cadets came from neighborhoods with significantly higher unemployment, on average, and lower youth labor force participation. We present supporting evidence in Table A.6. The overall unemployment rate is more than 1 percentage point higher, and the youth unemployment rate is more than 2 percentage points higher in the zip codes that non-White cadets come from compared with zip codes that White cadets come from. Interestingly, however, the overall labor force participation is higher in zip codes that non-White cadets come from. This all further supports the observation that non-White cadets come from zip codes with fewer economic opportunities and may need additional or different supports than White cadets receive.

For youth labor force participation and unemployment, there is some evidence of trends over time, although the magnitude of these changes is not too strong. After 2018 or 2019, cadet neighborhoods' youth labor force participation increased and youth unemployment rates decreased, on average, suggesting that the program may be recruiting those from less economically stressed backgrounds, on average. Unlike the poverty measures, these trends appeared regardless of race and ethnicity or gender. However, as with the poverty measures, they further highlight a trend that the Youth ChalleNGe program should monitor to see whether it is systematically struggling to recruit from more-disadvantaged neighborhoods.

TABLE A.6

Differences in Youth ChalleNGe Cadet Labor Force Outcomes, by Race and Ethnicity and Gender

Zip Code–Level Variable	Male Cadets' Zip Codes	Female Cadets' Zip Codes	White Cadets' Zip Codes	Non-White Cadets' Zip Codes	All U.S. Zip Codes (Weighted by Population)
Labor force participation	0.617 (0.082)*	0.622 (0.080)	0.604 (0.089)*	0.629 (0.075)	0.635 (0.082)
Youth labor force participation	0.580 (0.115)	0.582 (0.112)	0.586 (0.128)*	0.576 (0.102)	0.593 (0.114)
Unemployment rate	0.063 (0.038)*	0.064 (0.037)	0.056 (0.036)*	0.069 (0.037)	0.055 (0.029)
Youth unemployment rate	0.135 (0.094)	0.135 (0.091)	0.122 (0.096)*	0.144 (0.090)	0.118 (0.078)

SOURCES: Authors' calculations from RAND annual collections, Youth ChalleNGe classes including 2016–2021; ACS five-year averages, 2016–2020 (U.S. Census Bureau, 2022); and Opportunity Insights data (Opportunity Insights, undated). These sources are described in more detail at the beginning of this appendix.

NOTE: Asterisks denote significant differences between group averages by race and ethnicity or gender at $p < 0.05$.

Additional Tests for Robustness

In addition to the main analyses described above, we also conducted several robustness tests. We assessed the robustness of the results found for all cadets to see whether they also held for graduates (roughly 75 percent of the full sample). We also tested to see whether trends or differences still remained when removing 2020 and 2021 cohorts from the analyses, given that recruitment and program operations were substantially affected by the COVID-19 pandemic. Results are presented in Table A.7.

While there are small changes in the magnitudes of different results, the overall trends still remain. Generally, graduates from the Youth ChalleNGe program came from zip codes with slightly higher levels of economic connectedness, slightly higher median family income, and slightly lower poverty rates. The magnitudes of these differences are much smaller than the magnitudes of the differences between Youth ChalleNGe cadets and the U.S. or non–Youth ChalleNGe average. There were no substantial differences in overall averages after removing 2020 and 2021 cohorts from our sample. The pattern of differences by race and ethnicity and gender were also nearly identical in both subsets to the full analytic sample.

Among the regression results, some time trends were no longer statistically significant after removing 2020 and 2021 from the sample. Trends over time in the rate of public assistance use, unemployment rates, and youth unemployment rates are no longer distinguishable from zero, suggesting that at least some of the changes in the types of areas that cadets came from were driven by recruitment changes during the pandemic year. Nonetheless, larger, more substantial time trends in variables related to household and child poverty rates were still significant in the reduced samples.

TABLE A.7

Youth ChalleNGe Cadets Compared with U.S. Average and Robustness Checks for Non-Pandemic Years and Only Youth ChalleNGe Graduates

Zip Code–Level Variable	All Youth ChalleNGe Cadets' Zip Codes	Non-Pandemic-Year Cadets' Zip Codes	Youth ChalleNGe Graduates' Zip Codes	All U.S. Zip Codes (Weighted by Population)
Economic connectedness	0.786 (0.194)*	0.782 (0.194)*	0.796 (0.194)*	0.869 (0.229)
Clustering	0.099 (0.020)*	0.099 (0.020)*	0.099 (0.019)*	0.095 (0.016)
Volunteer rates	0.064 (0.031)*	0.063 (0.031)*	0.065 (0.031)*	0.066 (0.030)
Civic organizations	0.013 (0.013)*	0.013 (0.013)*	0.013 (0.012)*	0.015 (0.020)
Percentage White	0.624 (0.262)*	0.614 (0.264)*	0.631 (0.257)*	0.704 (0.222)
Percentage foreign-born	0.096 (0.106)*	0.097 (0.107)*	0.102 (0.110)*	0.135 (0.127)
Percentage with less than a high school education	0.134 (0.085)*	0.135 (0.084)*	0.134 (0.088)*	0.117 (0.087)
Percentage living in crowded households	0.040 (0.051)*	0.040 (0.051)*	0.042 (0.053)*	0.036 (0.043)
Median income ($)	60,670 (21,568)*	60,445 (21,655)*	61,907 (21,706)*	70,753 (28,795)
Household poverty rate	0.149 (0.082)*	0.151 (0.082)*	0.145 (0.080)*	0.126 (0.078)
Child poverty rate	0.183 (0.121)*	0.186 (0.122)*	0.177 (0.118)*	0.146 (0.110)
Percentage using public assistance	0.028 (0.025)*	0.028 (0.026)*	0.028 (0.025)*	0.025 (0.021)
Labor force participation	0.618 (0.082)*	0.619 (0.082)*	0.620 (0.081)*	0.635 (0.082)
Youth labor force participation	0.581 (0.114)*	0.579 (0.114)*	0.581 (0.113)*	0.593 (0.114)
Unemployment rate	0.063 (0.037)*	0.064 (0.037)*	0.062 (0.036)*	0.055 (0.029)
Youth unemployment rate	0.135 (0.093)*	0.136 (0.093)*	0.132 (0.092)*	0.118 (0.078)

SOURCES: Authors' calculations from RAND annual collections, Youth ChalleNGe classes including 2016–2021; ACS five-year averages, 2016–2020 (U.S. Census Bureau, 2022); and Opportunity Insights data (Opportunity Insights, undated). These sources are described in more detail at the beginning of this appendix.

NOTE: Asterisks denote significant differences between ChalleNGe cadets' zip codes and the U.S. averages at $p < 0.05$.

Long-Term Outcome Supplemental Materials

Overview of Statewide Longitudinal Data Systems Data

We received 14 data files from GA•AWARDS. These files were delivered to RAND from GOSA using GOSA's secure FTP (file transfer protocol) site. The files include information on students' K–12 education (provided by the Georgia Department of Education), postsecondary education (provided by the University System of Georgia, the Technical College System of Georgia, the Georgia Independent College System, and the National Student Clearinghouse), labor force participation (provided by the Georgia Department of Labor), and ChalleNGe participation (provided by the Georgia ChalleNGe sites).

For each SY from 2010–2011 through 2018–2019, we received the following types of data:

- K–12 education institutions: year, school district, school ID, school name, charter status, Title I eligibility
- postsecondary institutions: year, institution name, institution ID, type of institution (two-year or four-year program), state of institution
- ChalleNGe program participation: student ID, program start date, indicator for Youth ChalleNGe completion, date of Youth ChalleNGe completion, indicator for Job ChalleNGe completion, date of Job ChalleNGe completion
- student demographics: year, student ID, age, grade level, gender, race and ethnicity, indicators for ELS status, SWD status, gifted program enrollment, FRPL eligibility, migrant status, housing status, dual-enrollment status
- student K–12 enrollment: year, student ID, school ID, school entry code, grade level, days present, days absent (including disaggregation by excused or unexcused status), school exit reason code
- student K–12 assessment: year, student ID, school ID, test date, test identifier, test score, performance level
- student discipline: year, student ID, school ID, event description and code, disciplinary action description, length of suspension in days

- student postsecondary enrollment: school term, student ID, institution ID, academic program description, academic major or program, age at enrollment, cumulative grade point average, corresponding degree level
- student postsecondary attainment: school term, student ID, institution ID, academic program description, degree awarded, age at degree award, academic major or program, Classification of Instructional Programs code, and whether the program was a science, technology, engineering, or math field
- labor force participation: fiscal quarter of wages earned, student ID, North American Industry Classification System code, Standard Industrial Classification code, wage amount.

Facilitating a Linkage Between Statewide Longitudinal Data Systems and ChalleNGe Data

The Georgia ChalleNGe program facilitated the connection with the state SLDS. Program leadership prepared a data file that included key information about Youth and Job ChalleNGe program participants, including the individual's name, date of birth, race and ethnicity, gender, last known grade of enrollment, last known school of enrollment, ChalleNGe site, year of program participation, and whether the individual graduated Youth ChalleNGe and participated in or graduated from Job ChalleNGe. These data were securely transferred directly to staff at GOSA, who then merged these files with the SLDS. GOSA staff stripped all identifying information from the newly created files and then transferred the generated files to the research team. Of the 12,309 individuals with information in the ChalleNGe file, 1,388 were not able to be matched by GOSA.

Estimation Methodology for Impact Analysis

In this section, we describe the estimation methodology employed for research question 4: "To what extent do Georgia Youth and Job ChalleNGe participants experience different high school, postsecondary, and labor market outcomes relative to similar youth who did not participate in these programs?" We employ a quasi-experimental methodology known as *propensity score weighting* to control for observable differences between the intervention and comparison groups, similar to the method used in Mihaly, Arellano, and Prier (2022).

The study team was interested in the average treatment effect on the treated, or the effect of graduating from the Youth ChalleNGe program. This is represented by Equation B.1, with the underlying assumption represented by Equation B.2. In Equations B.1 and B.2, intervention T_i represents the treatment, which is whether the youth graduates from Youth ChalleNGe; $Y_i(1)$ denotes the potential outcome of student i had student i graduated from Youth ChalleNGe ($T_i = 1$); and $Y_i(0)$ denotes the potential outcome of student i had student i not participated in Youth ChalleNGe ($T_i = 0$). The average treatment effect (ATE) on the treated is defined as

$$ATE = E\big[Y_i(0) - Y_i(1)\big]. \tag{B.1}$$

For an individual student, both potential outcomes cannot be observed, so we constructed an appropriate counterfactual. The analysis assumes conditional independence—namely, that conditional on observable characteristics, denoted by X_i, the potential outcome under no intervention, $Y_i(0)$, is mean-independent of intervention T_i:

$$Y_i(0) \perp T_i \mid X_i. \tag{B.2}$$

The conditional independence assumption enters the analysis in two ways. First, we used X_i to estimate the propensity of graduating from Youth ChalleNGe (relative to not graduating from Youth ChalleNGe) and weight the observable characteristics of graduates from Youth ChalleNGe toward the observable characteristics of nongraduates. Second, the study team estimated propensity weights using the Toolkit for Weighting and Analysis of Nonequivalent Groups (TWANG) methodology (McCaffrey et al., 2013; Ridgeway et al., 2022). This method constructs a set of matching weights that uses machine learning methods to construct weights that minimize the difference between the treatment and weighted comparison groups.

The analysis proceeded in two steps. In the first step, we estimated the matching weights using the TWANG package. The estimation equation for the first stage is the following:

$$Prob(CHAL_i = 1) = \alpha + X'_{icsr}B + Z'_s\Gamma + \eta_c + \rho_r + \varepsilon_{icsr}, \tag{B.3}$$

where $Prob(CHAL_i = 1)$ is the probability that a youth graduates from Youth ChalleNGe, and X_{icsr} are the observable characteristics of youth i in the 8th-grade cohort c attending school s in region r of Georgia. The control variables included indicator for female, indicator for Latino, indicator for Black, indicator for SEH, indicator for FRPL eligibility, continuous measure of the number of days the student was absent in grade 8, continuous measure of the number of times the student was suspended in school, continuous measure of the number of times the student was suspended out of school, and continuous measure of scores on the grade 8 mathematics and English state standardized tests, standardized to have a mean of 0 and a standard deviation of 1 by SY. In addition to the student-level controls, we have school covariates denoted by Z_s that include school percentage Black, school percentage Latino, percentage of students in the school eligible for FRPL, school average scores on the mathematics and English state standardized tests, percentage of SEH in the school, number of suspensions in the school, indicator for whether the school is Title I, school average number of days students are absent, and an indicator that is 1 if the school has sent a student to Youth ChalleNGe in any of the prior SYs in our panel. We also include fixed effects for the 8th-grade cohort of the student (η_c) and for the region of the school (ρ_r). We conducted the analysis for all students with nonmissing data (also known as complete case analysis) and did not impute missing values.

Using TWANG 2.5 in R, we ran gradient-boosted logistic regression with 10,000 trees and a tree depth of 3 for each sample of analysis to create the propensity score weights. We created weights to estimate the ATE for our causal effect of interest in each model. Due to the size of our data and the computationally intensive nature of TWANG, we used a parameter to consider every third or fifth control iteration (depending on the size of the input data for the model) rather than optimizing over the entire set.

In the second step, we estimated a weighted regression using OLS:

$$Y_{icsr} = \gamma + \delta\, CHAL_{icsr} + X'_{icsr} K + Z'_s P + \eta_c + \rho_r + \omega_{icsr}, \tag{B.4}$$

where Y_{icsr} is the outcome measure of interest, $CHAL_{icsr}$ is an indicator for whether the youth graduates from Youth ChalleNGe, and the other controls are identical to the ones described in Equation B.3. The outcome measures analyzed are listed in Tables 4.3 and 4.4 in Chapter 4.

Supplemental Results

What Is the Distribution of Youth ChalleNGe Cadets Across Schools in Georgia?

Table B.1 displays the characteristics of schools that include no Youth ChalleNGe participants, characteristics of schools that include at least one Youth ChalleNGe participant, and the characteristics of all schools in Georgia. Generally, there are no meaningful differences between schools that send students to Youth ChalleNGe and those that do not, nor are there meaningful differences between schools that send students to Youth ChalleNGe and all schools in the state.

TABLE B.1

Average Characteristics of Schools With and Without Youth ChalleNGe Participants, Compared with All Schools in Georgia

Characteristic	School with No Youth ChalleNGe Participant	School with at Least One Youth ChalleNGe Participant	All Schools in Georgia
Charter	4%	2%	3%
Title I	55%	57%	56%
School percentage American Indian	0%	0%	0%
School percentage Asian	3%	2%	3%
School percentage Black	38%	47%	43%
School percentage Latino	12%	10%	11%
School percentage White	43%	38%	40%
School percentage FRPL eligible	60%	65%	63%
School percentage ELS	4%	3%	3%
School percentage SWD	14%	13%	14%
School percentage SEH	2%	2%	2%
School percentage in gifted program	9%	7%	8%
School enrollment	680	1,068	892
Percentage students with in-school suspension	14%	17%	16%
Percentage students with out-of-school suspension	10%	13%	12%
Average number of unexcused absences	3.46	5.12	4.37
Number of schools	504	609	1,113

How Do the 8th-Grade Background Characteristics and Behaviors of Youth ChalleNGe and Job ChalleNGe Graduates Compare with Non-ChalleNGe Graduates in Georgia?

In this section, we present the results of the statistical tests in comparing Youth ChalleNGe graduates with public school students in Georgia and comparing Job ChalleNGe graduates with public school students in Georgia. In Tables B.2 through B.4, if the Youth or Job ChalleNGe graduate average characteristic is statistically significantly different from the average characteristic for all students in Georgia, this is designated by an asterisk.

TABLE B.2
Student Demographics

Variable	Youth ChalleNGe	Job ChalleNGe	Georgia
Female gender	21*	26*	49
Black race	70*	69*	38
Latino ethnicity	6*	7*	12
White race	20*	20*	43
FRPL eligible	82*	79*	60
SEH	3*	3	2
SWD	20*	15	12
ELS	2*	2*	3
Gifted	2*	2*	13

NOTE: Asterisks indicate instances where the difference between the Youth or Job ChalleNGe average characteristic is statistically significantly different from the average characteristic for all public school students in Georgia at $p < 0.05$. N/A indicates not applicable; there were fewer than 10 graduates in the cell, and data are therefore suppressed.

TABLE B.3
Absence and Discipline

Variable	Youth ChalleNGe	Job ChalleNGe	Georgia
Proportion of days absent	6*	4	4
Any in-school suspension	47*	43*	17
Any out-of-school suspension	41*	33*	11

NOTE: Asterisks indicate instances where the difference between the Youth or Job ChalleNGe average characteristic is statistically significantly different from the average characteristic for all public school students in Georgia at $p < 0.05$. N/A indicates not applicable; there were fewer than 10 graduates in the cell, and data are therefore suppressed.

TABLE B.4
Standardized Test Scores

Variable	Youth ChalleNGe	Job ChalleNGe	Georgia
Math	−0.75*	−0.63*	0
English	−0.78*	−0.59*	0

NOTE: Asterisks indicate instances where the difference between the Youth or Job ChalleNGe average characteristic is statistically significantly different from the average characteristic for all public school students in Georgia at $p < 0.05$. N/A indicates not applicable; there were fewer than 10 graduates in the cell, and data are therefore suppressed.

How Do the Outcomes Among Youth and Jobs ChalleNGe Participants Compare with Each Other and with Non-ChalleNGe Graduates in Georgia?

In Tables B.5 through B.9, we present the results of the statistical tests in comparing Youth ChalleNGe graduates with public school students in Georgia and comparing Job ChalleNGe graduates with public school students in Georgia. In the following tables, if the Youth or Job ChalleNGe graduate average characteristic is statistically significantly different ($p < 0.05$) from the average characteristic for all students in Georgia, this is designated by an asterisk.

TABLE B.5

Credentials

Variable	Youth ChalleNGe	Job ChalleNGe	Georgia
Certificate, within 6 years	5*	44*	3
Certificate, within 7 years	4	34*	4
Certificate, within 8 years	5	N/A	5
Associate's degree, within 6 years	0*	0*	1
Associate's degree, within 7 years	0*	0*	2
Associate's degree, within 8 years	0*	N/A	3

NOTE: Asterisks indicate instances where the difference between the Youth or Job ChalleNGe average characteristic is statistically significantly different from the average characteristic for all public school students in Georgia at $p < 0.05$. N/A indicates not applicable; there were fewer than 10 graduates in the cell, and data are therefore suppressed.

TABLE B.6

Enrollment in Two-Year Institution

Variable	Youth ChalleNGe	Job ChalleNGe	Georgia
Enrollment in two-year institution, within 5 years	17*	64*	15
Enrollment in two-year institution, within 6 years	18*	74*	18
Enrollment in two-year institution, within 7 years	19*	72*	19
Enrollment in two-year institution, within 8 years	18*	N/A	19

NOTE: Asterisks indicate instances where the difference between the Youth or Job ChalleNGe average characteristic is statistically significantly different from the average characteristic for all public school students in Georgia at $p < 0.05$. N/A indicates not applicable; there were fewer than 10 graduates in the cell, and data are therefore suppressed.

TABLE B.7
Annual Wages

Variable	Youth ChalleNGe ($)	Job ChalleNGe ($)	Georgia ($)
Age 17–18	6,364*	6,343	5,657
Age 18–19	8,832	9,916	8,726
Age 19–20	10,876	11,535	11,143
Age 20–21	13,147	11,664	13,794
Age 21–22	12,781*	N/A	16,377

NOTE: Asterisks indicate instances where the difference between the Youth or Job ChalleNGe average characteristic is statistically significantly different from the average characteristic for all public school students in Georgia at $p < 0.05$. N/A indicates not applicable; there were fewer than 10 graduates in the cell, and data are therefore suppressed.

TABLE B.8
Total Earnings

Variable	Youth ChalleNGe ($)	Job ChalleNGe ($)	Georgia ($)
Age 17–18	6,611*	6,030	5,821
Age 18–19	10,850	10,580	10,503
Age 19–20	14,171*	13,701	14,956
Age 20–21	16,275*	15,165*	18,556
Age 21–22	16,868*	15,393*	20,672

NOTE: Asterisks indicate instances where the difference between the Youth or Job ChalleNGe average characteristic is statistically significantly different from the average characteristic for all public school students in Georgia at $p < 0.05$. N/A indicates not applicable; there were fewer than 10 graduates in the cell, and data are therefore suppressed.

TABLE B.9
Labor Force Participation

Variable	Youth ChalleNGe	Job ChalleNGe	Georgia
Age 17–18	81*	77*	66
Age 18–19	87*	86*	76
Age 19–20	89*	91*	81
Age 20–21	90*	91*	83
Age 21–22	91*	NA	85

NOTE: Asterisks indicate instances where the difference between the Youth or Job ChalleNGe average characteristic is statistically significantly different from the average characteristic for all public school students in Georgia at $p < 0.05$. N/A indicates not applicable; there were fewer than 10 graduates in the cell, and data are therefore suppressed.

What Is the Impact of Youth ChalleNGe on Postsecondary and Labor Force Outcomes?

Figures B.1 through B.11 illustrate how the propensity score weights reduce the difference, on average, between the treatment group (Youth ChalleNGe graduates) and the comparison group (non–Youth ChalleNGe graduates). To create these effect size plots, first we calculated the standardized mean difference for each covariate, which is the mean of the treatment group minus the mean of the comparison group divided by the pooled sample (treatment and comparison) standard deviation. On the left side of the plot, these standardized mean differences are shown prior to weighting, whereas on the right side of the plot, they are shown after weighting the comparison group with the weights calculated from the propensity score weighting model. Solid red circles indicate a statistically significant difference between the treatment and comparison group for a given covariate. Red lines indicate that the weighting increased the point estimate for the standardized mean difference, whereas light blue lines indicate that the standardized mean difference is lower. A basic rule of thumb to determine whether the weighting improved the balance between the treatment and comparison groups is if the standardized mean difference after weighting is below 0.25.

We ran separate weighting models for education and labor force outcomes, depending on the number of cohorts included in the analysis. Some of the analytic models use the same weights. For example, obtaining a certificate within six years uses the same weights as obtaining an associate's degree within six years. We present effect size plots for each weighting model in the following figures.

FIGURE B.1

Effect Size Difference Before and After Propensity Score Weighting, Education Outcomes, Within Five Years

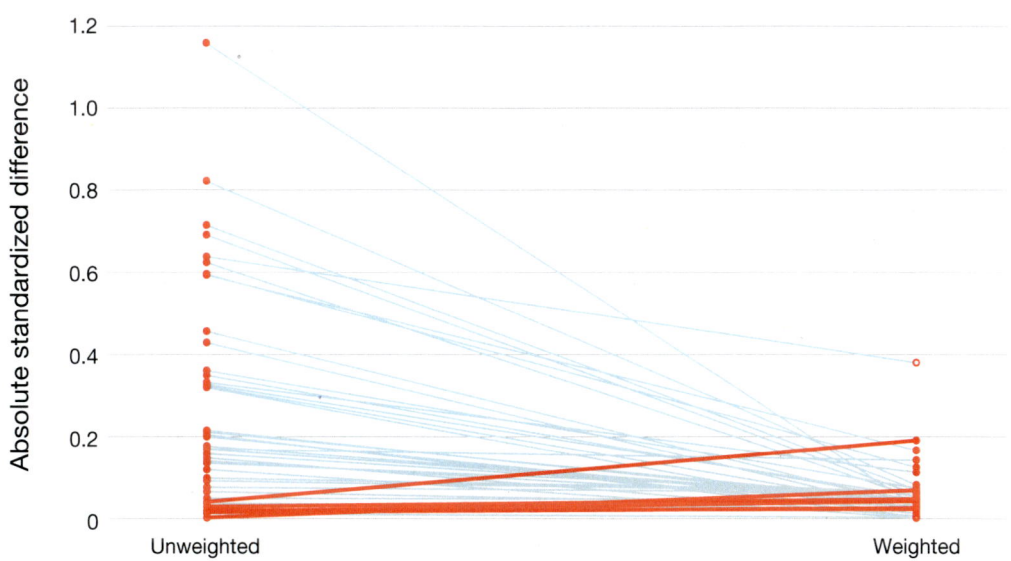

NOTE: Effect size difference is shown for education outcomes (enrollment in a two-year institution, attainment of a certificate, attainment of an associate's degree) for cohorts observed within five years of 8th grade (i.e., 2011, 2012, 2013, and 2014 cohorts).

FIGURE B.2

Effect Size Difference Before and After Propensity Score Weighting, Education Outcomes, Within Six Years

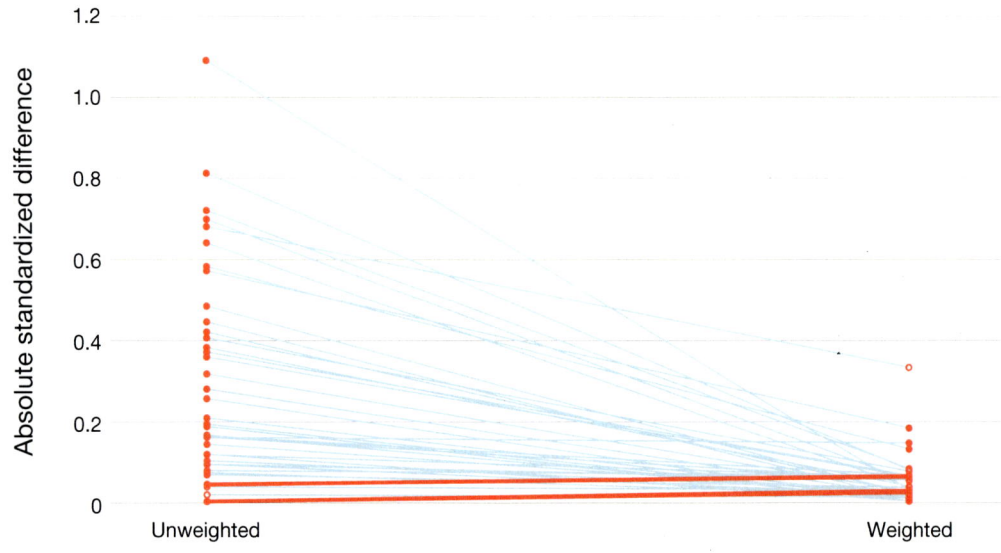

NOTE: Effect size difference is shown for education outcomes (enrollment in a two-year institution, attainment of a certificate, attainment of an associate's degree) for cohorts observed within six years of 8th grade (i.e., 2011, 2012, and 2013 cohorts).

FIGURE B.3

Effect Size Difference Before and After Propensity Score Weighting, Education Outcomes, Within Seven Years

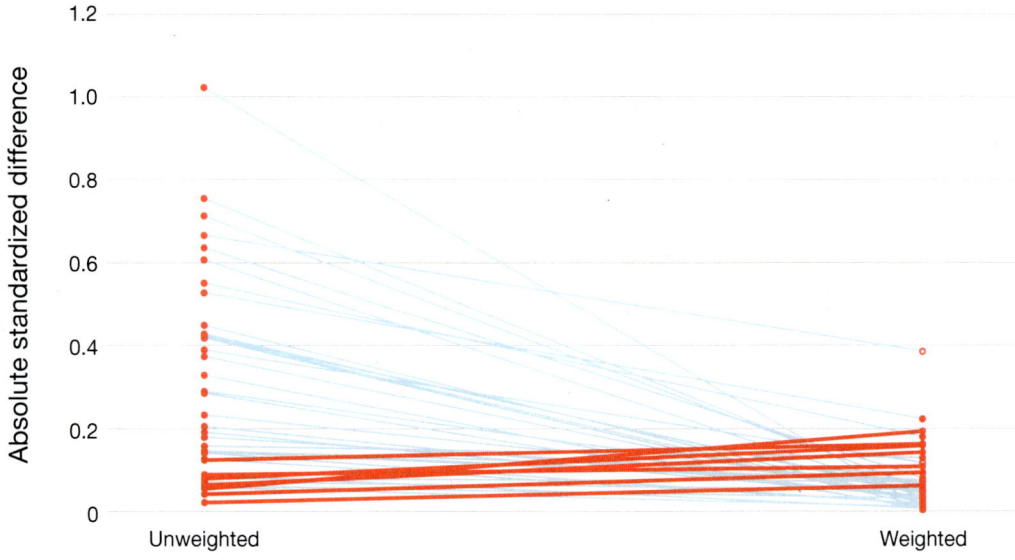

NOTE: Effect size difference is shown for education outcomes (enrollment in a two-year institution, attainment of a certificate, attainment of an associate's degree) for cohorts observed within seven years of 8th grade (i.e., 2011 and 2012 cohorts).

FIGURE B.4

Effect Size Difference Before and After Propensity Score Weighting, Education Outcomes, Within Eight Years

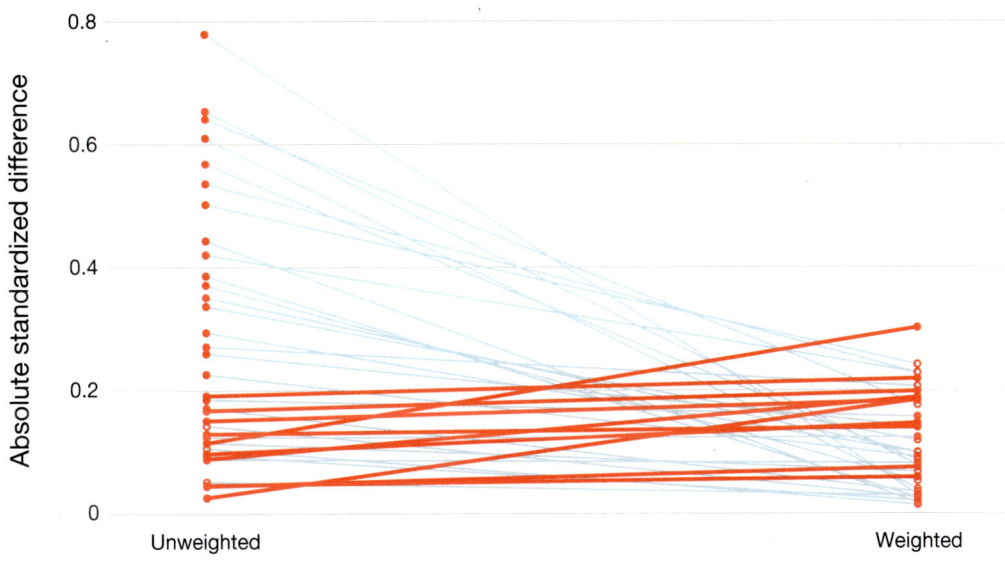

NOTE: Effect size difference is shown for education outcomes (enrollment in a two-year institution, attainment of a certificate, attainment of an associate's degree) for cohorts observed within eight years of 8th grade (i.e., 2011 cohort).

FIGURE B.5

Effect Size Difference Before and After Propensity Score Weighting, Labor Force Participation, All Years

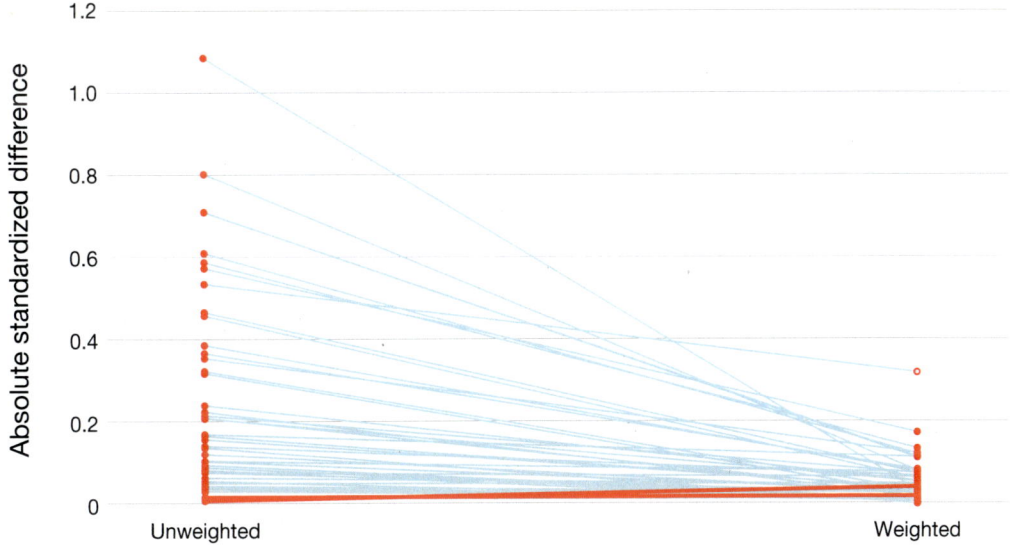

NOTE: Effect size difference is shown for labor force participation for all cohorts with 8th-grade data.

FIGURE B.6

Effect Size Difference Before and After Propensity Score Weighting, Annual Wages, Age 17–18

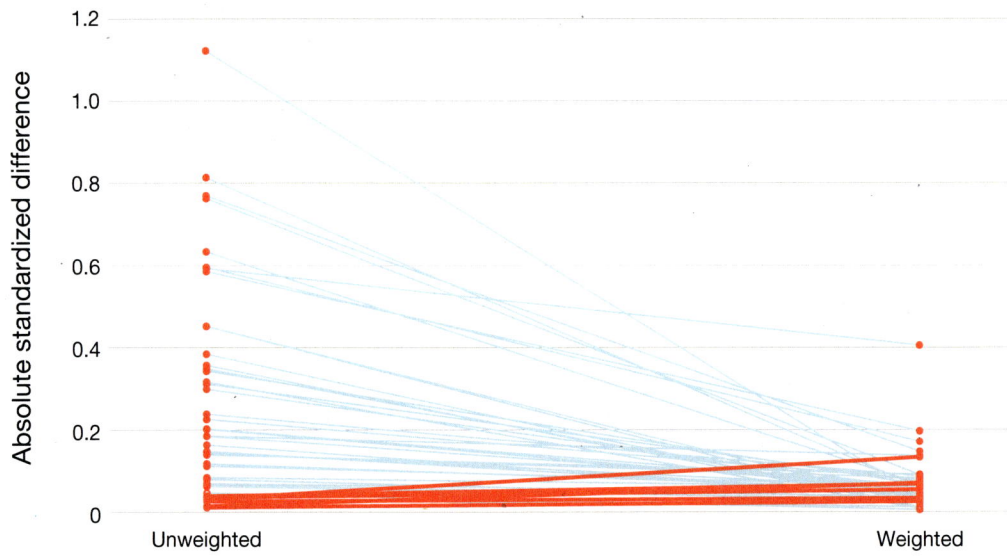

FIGURE B.7

Effect Size Difference Before and After Propensity Score Weighting, Annual Wages, Age 18–19

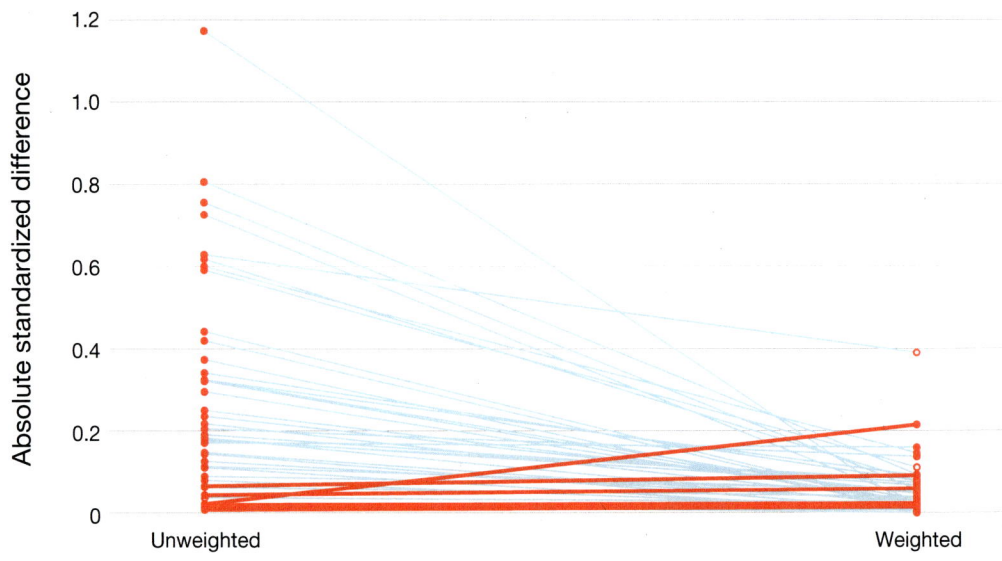

FIGURE B.8

Effect Size Difference Before and After Propensity Score Weighting, Annual Wages, Age 19–20

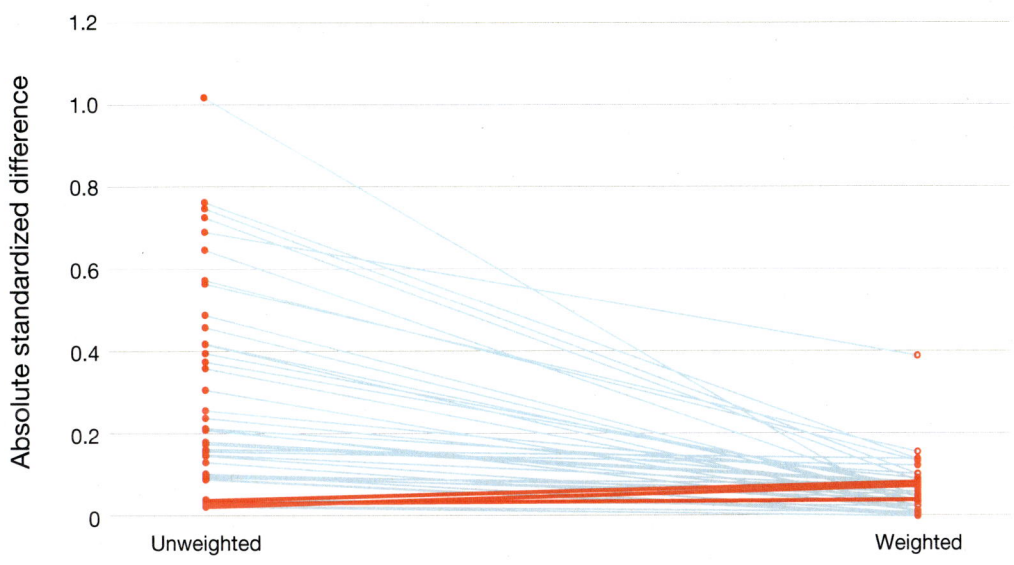

FIGURE B.9

Effect Size Difference Before and After Propensity Score Weighting, Annual Wages, Age 20–21

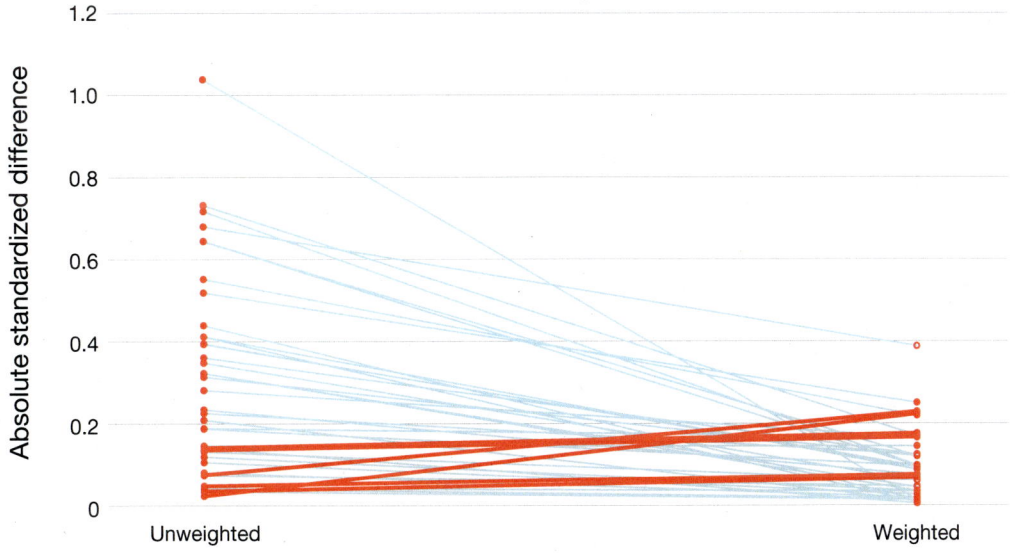

FIGURE B.10

Effect Size Difference Before and After Propensity Score Weighting, Annual Wages, Age 21–22

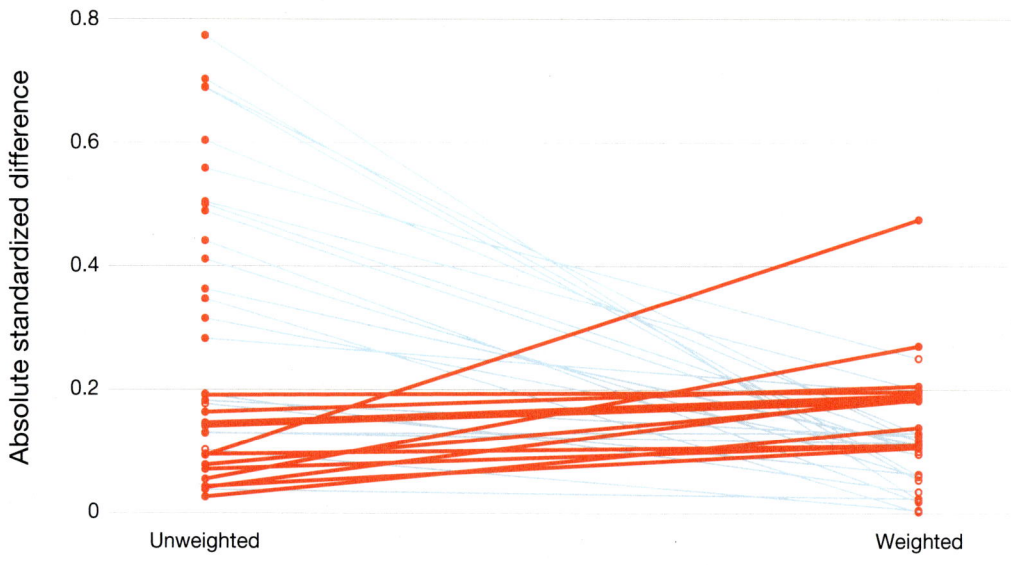

FIGURE B.11

Effect Size Difference Before and After Propensity Score Weighting, Total Earnings, All Ages

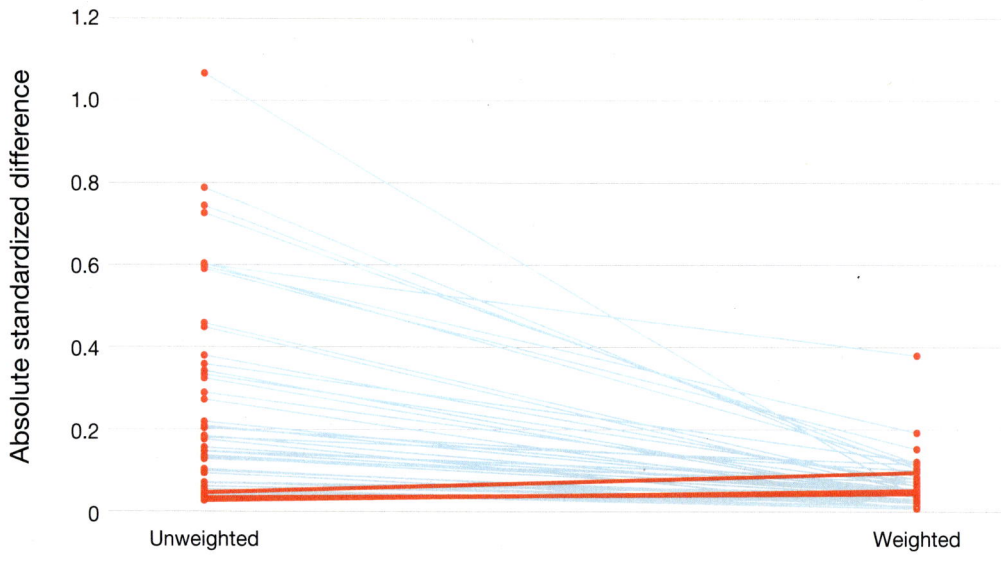

NOTE: Effect size difference is shown for total earnings for all cohorts with 8th-grade data.

Table B.10 displays the coefficient estimates, standard errors, R^2 regression fit statistic, total sample sizes, and sample sizes of the treated group for each of the impact estimation models. Each row presents information from a separate weighted regression, as described in Equation B.4 in the previous Estimation Methodology for Impact Analysis section.

TABLE B.10

Coefficient Estimates, Standard Errors, and Sample Sizes, Impact of Youth ChalleNGe

Outcome	Coefficient Estimate	Standard Error	R^2	N	N Treated
Enrollment in two-year institution, within 5 years	0.0328	0.0186	0.0666	378,992	1,692
Enrollment in two-year institution, within 6 years	−0.0034	0.0218	0.0433	282,067	1,135
Enrollment in two-year institution, within 7 years	0.0303	0.0306	0.0778	186,477	600
Enrollment in two-year institution, within 8 years	0.0286	0.0425	0.1071	91,659	168
Certificate, within 6 years	0.0431	0.0178	0.0678	282,067	1,135
Certificate, within 7 years	0.0415	0.0223	0.1223	186,477	600
Certificate, within 8 years	0.0787	0.0343	0.2087	91,659	168
Associate's degree, within 6 years	0.0023	0.0072	0.0458	282,067	1,135
Associate's degree, within 7 years	−0.0070	0.0098	0.0365	186,477	600
Associate's degree, within 8 years	−0.0263	0.0020	0.0247	91,659	168
Bachelor's degree, within 8 years	−0.0183	0.0201	0.0790	91,659	168
Labor force participation	0.096	0.013	0.198	660,994	3,344
Labor force participation at age 17–18	0.1222	0.0160	0.0541	481,176	2,302
Labor force participation at age 18–19	0.0925	0.0155	0.0477	378,992	1,692
Labor force participation at age 19–20	0.0637	0.0177	0.0384	282,067	1,135
Labor force participation at age 20–21	0.0521	0.0207	0.0527	186,477	600
Labor force participation at age 21–22	0.0571	0.0261	0.0491	91,659	168
Wage at age 17–18	87.59	292.71	0.0520	303,514	1,664
Wage at age 18–19	−737.88	352.62	0.0745	256,703	1,232
Wage at age 19–20	−748.18	613.86	0.0498	191,646	796

Table B.10—Continued

Outcome	Coefficient Estimate	Standard Error	R^2	N	N Treated
Wage at age 20–21	−3,943.17	1,082.75	0.1292	61,799	123
Wage at age 21–22	−3,943.17	1,082.75	0.1292	61,799	123
Total earnings at age 17–18	58.78	291.88	0.0765	468,314	2,628
Total earnings at age 18–19	−321.19	419.40	0.1271	468,314	2,628
Total earnings at age 19–20	−571.32	594.63	0.1706	468,314	2,628
Total earnings at age 20–21	−1,075.02	760.00	0.0310	468,314	2,628
Total earnings at age 21–22	−1,453.76	864.22	0.0443	468,314	2,628

Survey Development and Administration

To support the Job ChalleNGe outcomes study, the RAND team coordinated with administrators at each of the six Job ChalleNGe sites to field two types of surveys: (1) a *pre-post* survey and (2) a *long-term outcomes* survey. The pre-post survey was intended for current Job ChalleNGe participants to take at the beginning and end of the program's residential phase and focused on capturing individuals' self-esteem, life coping skills, and career and college self-efficacy. The long-term outcomes survey was designed for former Job ChalleNGe participants and focused on capturing individuals' participation in postsecondary education, the workforce, and civic activities since leaving Job ChalleNGe. This appendix details the purpose of the surveys, development of the survey instruments, training procedures for survey administration, survey response rates, and barriers encountered during development and administration.

Instrument Development

The process of collaborating with Job ChalleNGe sites to develop and administer the pre-post and long-term outcomes surveys served two purposes. First, the surveys were the primary, and often sole, data collection method on several proximate and distal outcomes of interest to the Job ChalleNGe study. The pre-post surveys were designed to capture individuals' self-reported levels on a number of theoretically proximate outcomes (e.g., self-esteem, life coping skills, career and college self-efficacy) at the beginning (*pre* survey) and end (*post* survey) of their participation in the residential phase of Job ChalleNGe. The pre-post surveys provided a unique opportunity to systematically gather individual data on dispositions and skills not captured in existing program data. The long-term outcomes surveys were designed to allow former Job ChalleNGe participants (including those who completed and those who did not complete Job ChalleNGe) to self-report on their post-ChalleNGe participation in postsecondary education, the workforce, and civic activities, such as voting and volunteering. For sites in states without linkable administrative data, responses to the long-term outcomes survey would serve as the sole source of information on the postsecondary and workforce outcomes of former Job ChalleNGe participants. Long-term outcomes survey responses would still be valuable even for sites in states with linkable administrative data, as the information gathered through the survey would likely be more detailed (e.g., job titles, availability of benefits) than what would be available through administrative databases (e.g., annual wages).

Second, this data collection served as a way to assess and develop sites' capacity for data collection. Staff at Job ChalleNGe possessed a variety of experience with collecting participant data. At a minimum, several sites indicated that they did not collect participant data beyond what was required by Cadet Tracker. Some sites reported that they conducted exit surveys with participants to gather feedback on the program, but that the data collected from these exit surveys were not digitized or maintained for future analysis. Administering the pre-post and long-term outcomes surveys required sites to develop several new capacities, including (1) managing rosters of Job ChalleNGe participants across multiple classes, (2) maintaining crosswalks that allow linking across multiple types of participant identifiers, (3) deploying a survey and tracking responses at multiple time points, and (4) transferring data to external research partners. Participation in survey data collection gave sites an opportunity to develop capacities that are transferrable to future data collection and analysis efforts.

Instrument Development Process

Both the pre-post survey and long-term outcomes survey were developed using a three-step procedure: (1) producing an initial draft within the RAND evaluation team, (2) gathering comments and feedback from individual Job ChalleNGe sites on this initial draft, and (3) producing a final draft that consolidates recommendations from the individual Job ChalleNGe sites.

Members of the RAND evaluation team shared the initial draft of the surveys with site leadership and conducted site-specific meetings to provide an overview of survey content and gather immediate feedback on survey domains and items; sites were given additional time following these meetings to provide feedback after additional review. Program staff feedback typically were suggestions to modify language used to describe program tracks or components to match the terminology used by the sites themselves. Other, less common types of site feedback included suggesting the removal of survey items related to factors that site staff stated were unlikely to vary across participants or change throughout the duration of the residential phase (e.g., nutrition) and flagging items related to self-esteem that site staff identified as having had the potential to trigger emotional duress among participants. After meeting with each of the six Job ChalleNGe sites, we produced a final version of each survey that consolidated any feedback provided by site leadership. This final version was recirculated to site leadership to provide opportunity for minor edits and revisions prior to survey programming.

Preparing for Survey Administration

Members of the RAND evaluation team did not have access to personally identifiable information of Job ChalleNGe participants. Therefore, the RAND team worked closely with leadership at each Job ChalleNGe site to plan and conduct survey administration. Each site identified a staff member or members who would be responsible for administering each survey. With these individuals, we discussed the specific responsibilities required of each site to administer the survey and detailed steps and timelines for administering each survey.

Selecting Site Survey Administrators

Across sites, the initial step was identifying the person or people who would serve as a survey administrator for that site and as a point of contact for the research team. All sites initially selected one staff member to serve as their survey administrator. Because survey administration was a novel responsibility across most sites, the existing role of that survey administrator differed across sites; formal job titles of survey administrators included counselors, placement coordinators, and program directors.

Selecting a Survey Platform

To ease the administrative burden on each site, RAND researchers programmed each survey and produced a detailed guide on how to administer the survey on both a free (Google Forms) and paid (SurveyMonkey) platform. Both survey platforms provided similar functionality with regard to survey item formats, survey skip logic, and data export options. However, SurveyMonkey, relative to Google Forms, provided a number of advantages that would be beneficial to sites in administering the survey, including, crucially, the ability to upload and maintain student rosters on the SurveyMonkey platform, the ability to send out emails directly within the platform, and the ability to easily track and remind nonrespondents to complete the survey. Five of the six sites opted to use SurveyMonkey to deploy the surveys. All sites were provided with a copy of each survey and a detailed administration guide for the platform they chose.

Producing a Crosswalk

A challenging aspect of administering the surveys was providing sites with a method for sending deidentified data to RAND. This process is additionally difficult in the case of the pre-post surveys, which required that sites maintain a consistent identifier across the pre and the post survey that would allow the evaluation team to match individuals' responses from both surveys. To do so, we provided site survey administrators with a template for a crosswalk file that would be used to (1) identify the sample of Job ChalleNGe participants to be surveyed and (2) assign a unique identifier for each student that would be used only for the purposes of this study. This template identified the fields that survey administrators would have to fill out (e.g., email address, name) in addition to a basic ID format that sites could use to assign unique identifiers (e.g., JC_SC_0001, JC_SC_0002). We asked survey administrators to fill out a crosswalk for each class prior to the administration of the pre survey and emphasized the importance of keeping participants' generated IDs consistent across administrations of the survey.

Because we did not need to link the long-term outcomes survey responses to other data sources, we opted to make it anonymous, eliminating the need for administrators to assign participants unique identifiers. This was intended to reduce administrative burden on the sites.

Deploying the Survey

Both Google Forms (with modification) and SurveyMonkey offer options to send out surveys either through generating a universal URL (i.e., the same survey link for each participant) or through sending out participant-specific URLs via email. In the guides provided to survey administrators, we strongly recommended that administrators send participant-specific URLs via email. The primary reason for this preference is that sending participants individualized survey links that were pre-associated with the unique identifier created for them obviates the need for participants to remember and accurately input their unique identifier into the survey when completing it. This is especially important given that there could be up to five months between the administration of the pre and post survey, which could lead to forgotten ID numbers.

For the long-term outcomes survey, which did not require sites to assign unique identifiers, sites were encouraged to generate a universal URL, which they could distribute in media (e.g., email, text message, Facebook group) of their choice.

Transferring Data to RAND

Finally, sites were instructed on how to send collected responses back to RAND using a secure data transfer portal (Kiteworks). To avoid the transfer of personally identifiable information, sites were provided with specific export options for both Google Forms and SurveyMonkey that would omit any personally identifiable information from the exported results and were instructed to review the exported file for identifiable information prior to uploading it to Kiteworks.

Survey Administration and Response

The pre-post surveys were administered between fall 2021 and spring 2022 at the Job ChalleNGe sites. The long-term outcomes survey was administered in late spring 2022 to individuals who participated in Job ChalleNGe in spring 2021. In Tables C.1 and C.2, we provide an overview of the number of participants invited to participate in a survey and the number of completed surveys.

TABLE C.1

Count of Pre-Post Survey Invitations and Completions, by Site and Administration

Class	Site	Class Enrollment (Graduates)	Completed Pre Surveys	Completed Post Surveys	Pre-Post Surveys with Linked IDs[a]
Fall 2021	California	71 (5)	69	47	47
	Georgia	43 (26)	36	2	2
	Louisiana	Not provided	21	6	0
	Michigan	55 (31)	21	16	10
	South Carolina	22 (16)	14	Not provided	N/A
	West Virginia	30 (22)	16	12	12
Spring 2022	California	73 (48)	57	46	12
	Georgia	61 (45)	71	19	16
	Louisiana	Not provided	Not provided	3	N/A
	Michigan	56 (47)	47	32	29
	South Carolina	50 (34)	Not provided	Not provided	N/A
	West Virginia	38 (32)	20	11	8

NOTE: Class enrollment and graduate counts are drawn from data that each program provides to the National Guard Bureau each fiscal year. Because Louisiana's program was funded by the Department of Labor, rather than DoD, we do not have data on this program's enrollment and graduates. N/A = not applicable.

[a] While survey IDs linked pre and post responses, RAND's review of these data suggests that there are cases in which different individuals used the same ID, making the linkages moot.

TABLE C.2

Count of Long-Term Outcomes Survey Invitations and Completions, by Site and Administration

	Long-Term Outcomes Survey	
Site	Invited	Completed
California	Unknown	Not provided
Georgia	Unknown	5
Louisiana	Unknown	Not provided
Michigan	Unknown	9
South Carolina	34	Not provided
West Virginia	Unknown	Not administered

NOTE: This survey was administered in spring 2022 to individuals who participated in Job ChalleNGe in the spring 2021 class cycle.

Barriers to Implementation

As can be deciphered by examining the counts of survey responses we received over the course of our various survey administrations and the number of pre-post survey responses that could be linked to assess change over time, these collections were fraught with challenges. We categorize these challenges into four types: staff capacity, maintenance of ID crosswalks, structuring survey administration, and lack of information on program graduates.

Staff Capacity

As discussed in Chapter 3, many Job ChalleNGe sites are experience staffing vacancies. These vacancies create additional workload and responsibilities for the staff who are actively supporting the program. During the time frame in which RAND collaborated with Job ChalleNGe programs on survey administration, we witnessed multiple staff positions turn over or staff get called away for military training assignments. When these temporary or permanent leaves of absence occurred, other program staff did not have the awareness, preparation, or training to support survey administration. There were also instances in which the survey was administered, the administrating staff member departed, and the remaining staff members did not have account login information to access and share collected responses with RAND. Our impression was that many job responsibilities sit solely with a single individual; when that person is unavailable, auxiliary tasks, such as data collection, are deprioritized in favor of more-critical program functions (e.g., cadet safety and well-being). Of note, these issues are not entirely unique to Job ChalleNGe, but they are issues that will need to be considered should site-level staff be tasked with collecting data on longer-term outcomes in the future.

Maintenance of Unique Identifiers

The Job ChalleNGe staff members working with RAND had no prior experience in establishing unique identifiers and maintaining those identifiers over the period of a class cycle. Individuals leading data collection have the critical responsibility of maintaining high-quality ID crosswalks that ensure the fidelity and utility of the data collected. Staff leading these tasks need to document and outline processes and decisions made in the ID crosswalk process; such materials help transition this task from one person to another within an organization, especially when those transitions happen between survey administrations. Unfortunately, the baseline training and guidance that we provided and the support offered during the administration period did not prevent issues with developing and using ID crosswalks. Should Job ChalleNGe or Youth ChalleNGe staff become responsible for systematic data collection procedures, staff will need additional training to ensure they possess the full set of skills needed for each type of data collection.

Structuring Survey Administration with Participant Schedules

While each Job ChalleNGe site operates a five-and-a-half-month residential phase class cycle, some of the technical training programs that individual sites offer do not begin or end with the first or last day of the class cycle. We observed that Job ChalleNGe sites were less likely to gather survey data from participants who had mid-cycle entry or exit dates. Additionally, sites established different procedures for administering the survey. For example, some sites established time for all Job ChalleNGe participants to take the survey together in the first few days of the program. Other sites sent an email to cadets and expected them to complete this survey during their downtime. These methods had different rates of survey completion, with the preset time in the participants' schedules being more generative. An important practice moving forward for sites integrating data collection into their regular practice will be to establish an administration or collection schedule that includes either time set aside for participants to answer surveys or a calendar of reminders and outreach to improve data collection rates.

Lack of Participant Contact Information

The long-term outcomes survey was intended to reach individuals who participated in Job ChalleNGe a full calendar year prior to survey administration. However, we heard from most of the Job ChalleNGe sites that they do not maintain contact information for former participants. The implications of this are numerous. First, the surveys cannot reach the intended population of individuals without current ways of contacting them. Second, the data that are collected may not accurately reflect the full set of individuals who participated in the program if there is systematic missingness in the contact information (e.g., younger participants, male compared with female students). Third, there is a cost associated with collecting data (e.g., staff time, survey software); many of these resources are expended regardless of how many individuals provide data, which increases the per-participant cost when key input data are not available.

Abbreviations

ACS	American Community Survey
ATE	average treatment effect
COVID-19	coronavirus disease 2019
CTE	career and technical education
DoD	U.S. Department of Defense
ELA	English/language arts
ELS	English learner student
FRPL	free or reduced-price lunch
GA•AWARDS	Georgia's Academic and Workforce Analysis and Research Data System
GED	General Educational Development
GOSA	Georgia Governor's Office of Student Achievement
HiSET	High School Equivalency Test
OLS	ordinary least squares
P-RAP	Post-Residential Action Plan
SEH	students experiencing homelessness
SES	socioeconomic status
SLDS	Statewide Longitudinal Data System
SWD	students with disabilities
SY	school year
TWANG	Toolkit for Weighting and Analysis of Nonequivalent Groups

References

Autor, David H., "Skills, Education, and the Rise of Earnings Inequality Among the '"Other 99 Percent,"' *Science*, Vol. 344, No. 6186, May 23, 2014.

Booher-Jennings, Jennifer, "Below the Bubble: 'Educational Triage' and the Texas Accountability System," *American Educational Research Journal*, Vol. 42, No. 2, January 2005.

Boustan, Leah Platt, "*Racial Residential Segregation in American Cities*," NBER Working Paper 19045, National Bureau of Economic Research, May 2013.

Cameron, Stephen V., and James J. Heckman, "The Nonequivalence of High School Equivalents," *Journal of Labor Economics*, Vol. 11, No. 1, Part 1, January 1993.

Carver, Priscilla Rouse, Laurie Lewis, and Peter Tice, *Alternative Schools and Programs for Public School Students at Risk of Educational Failure: 2007–08*, NCES 2010-026, National Center for Education Statistics, U.S. Department of Education, 2010.

Chetty, Raj, Matthew O. Jackson, Theresa Kuchler, Johannes Stroebel, Nathaniel Hendren, Robert B. Fluegge, Sara Gong, Federico Gonzalez, Armelle Grondin, Matthew Jacob, et al., "Social Capital I: Measurement and Associations with Economic Mobility," *Nature*, Vol. 608, No. 7921, August 4, 2022.

Constant, Louay, Robert Bozick, Nicholas Broten, and Joy S. Moini, *Examining Career and Technical Education in National Guard Youth ChalleNGe Programs*, RAND Corporation, RR-A271-4, 2021. As of August 2, 2023:
https://www.rand.org/pubs/research_reports/RRA271-4.html

Corte, Colleen, and Lisa Sontag-Padilla, *Goal-Setting to Support Cadet Success: Insights and Recommendations for the National Guard Youth ChalleNGe Program*, RAND Corporation, RR-A271-6, 2021. As of August 4, 2023:
https://www.rand.org/pubs/research_reports/RRA271-6.html

de Brey, Cristobal, Anlan Zhang, and Sarah Duffy, *Digest of Education Statistics 2020*, National Center for Education Statistics, Institute of Education Sciences, U.S. Department of Education, 2022.

Education Commission of the States, "50-State Comparison: Statewide Longitudinal Data Systems," webpage, December 14, 2021. As of March 11, 2024:
https://www.ecs.org/state-longitudinal-data-systems

Edwards, Kathryn A., Melanie A. Zaber, and Daniel Schwam, *What Are the Skills Required to Obtain a Good Job? An Analysis of Labor Markets, Occupational Features, and Skill Training for the Youth ChalleNGe Program*, RAND Corporation, RR-A271-3, 2022. As of August 4, 2023:
https://www.rand.org/pubs/research_reports/RRA271-3.html

Foote, Andrew, and Kevin M. Stange, *Attrition from Administrative Data: Problems and Solutions with an Application to Postsecondary Education*, Working Paper 30232, National Bureau of Economic Research, July 2022.

Georgia Department of Education, "Regional Education Service Agencies (RESAs)," webpage, undated. As of February 14, 2024:
https://www.gadoe.org/Pages/Regional-Education-Service-Agencies-(RESAs).aspx

Harris, Douglas N., Lihan Liu, Nathan Barrett, and Ruoxi Li, *Is the Rise of High School Graduation Rates Real? High-Stakes School Accountability and Strategic Behavior*, Annenberg Institute at Brown University, EdWorkingPaper No. 20-210, March 2020.

Kleiner, Brian, Rebecca Porch, and Elizabeth Farris, *Public Alternative Schools and Programs for Students at Risk of Education Failure: 2000–01*, NCES 2002-004, National Center for Education Statistics, U.S. Department of Education, September 2002.

Krieg, John M., "Are Students Left Behind? The Distributional Effects of the No Child Left Behind Act," *Education Finance and Policy*, Vol. 3, No. 2, April 2008.

Li, Fan, Kari Lock Morgan, and Alan M. Zaslavsky, "Balancing Covariates via Propensity Score Weighting," *Journal of the American Statistical Association*, Vol. 113, No. 521, 2018.

McCaffrey, Daniel F., Beth Ann Griffin, Daniel Almirall, Mary Ellen Slaughter, Rajeev Ramchand, and Lane F. Burgette, "A Tutorial on Propensity Score Estimation for Multiple Treatments Using Generalized Boosted Models," *Statistics in Medicine*, Vol. 32, No. 19, August 2013.

Mihaly, Kata, Brenda Arellano, and Shannon Prier, *Biliteracy Seals in a Large Urban District in New Mexico: Who Earns Them and How Do They Impact College Outcomes? Appendixes*, REL 2023-140, Regional Educational Laboratory Southwest, December 2022.

Millenky, Megan, Dan Bloom, Sara Muller-Ravett, and Joseph Broadus, *Staying on Course: Three-Year Results of the National Guard Youth ChalleNGe Evaluation*, MDRC, June 2011.

Mortimer, Jeylan T., *Working and Growing Up in America*, Harvard University Press, 2003.

National Center for Juvenile Justice, *Juvenile Arrest Rates by Offense, Sex, and Race (1980–2020)*, July 8, 2022.

National Guard Youth ChalleNGe Program, *2015 Performance and Accountability Highlights*, National Guard Bureau, December 2015.

Neal, Derek, and Diane Whitmore Schanzenbach, "Left Behind by Design: Proficiency Counts and Test-Based Accountability," *Review of Economics and Statistics*, Vol. 92, No. 2, May 2010.

Opportunity Insights, "Social Capital Atlas," webpage, undated. As of February 13, 2024:
https://socialcapital.org

Perez-Arce, Francisco, Louay Constant, David S. Loughran, and Lynn A. Karoly, *A Cost-Benefit Analysis of the National Guard Youth ChalleNGe Program*, RAND Corporation, TR-1193-NGYF, 2012. As of July 27, 2023:
http://www.rand.org/pubs/technical_reports/TR1193.html

Price, Hugh B., "Foundations, Innovation and Social Change: A Quixotic Journey Turned Case Study," working paper prepared during a practitioner residency, Rockefeller Foundation Bellagio Center, July 2010. As of January 20, 2022:
https://web.archive.org/web/20220120194547/http://cspcs.sanford.duke.edu/sites/default/files/Foundations%20Innovation%20and%20Social%20Change.pdf

Public Law 107-110, No Child Left Behind Act of 2001, January 8, 2002.

Ridgeway, Greg, Daniel F. McCaffrey, Andrew R. Morral, Matthew Cefalu, Lane F. Burgette, Joseph D. Pane, and Beth Ann Griffin, *Toolkit for Weighting and Analysis of Nonequivalent Groups: A Tutorial for the R TWANG Package*, RAND Corporation, TL-A570-5, 2022. As of May 3, 2024:
https://www.rand.org/pubs/tools/TLA570-5.html

Stetser, Marie C., and Robert Stillwell, *Public High School Four-Year On-Time Graduation Rates and Event Dropout Rates: School Years 2010–11 and 2011–12—First Look*, NCES 2014-391, National Center for Education Statistics, U.S. Department of Education, April 2014.

Substance Abuse and Mental Health Services Administration, *Key Substance Use and Mental Health Indicators in the United States: Results from the 2021 National Survey on Drug Use and Health*, HHS Publication No. PEP22-07-01-005, NSDUH Series H-57, Center for Behavioral Health Statistics and Quality, Substance Abuse and Mental Health Services Administration, 2022.

Taylor, Paul, and Richard Fry, *The Rise of Residential Segregation by Income*, Pew Social and Demographic Trends, Pew Research Center, 2012.

U.S. Bureau of Labor Statistics, "Total Unemployment Rate Unemployment Rate—Less than a High School Diploma, 16 to 19 years [LHSD1619]," webpage, Federal Reserve Bank of St. Louis, undated. As of November 15, 2023:
https://fred.stlouisfed.org/series/LHSD1619

U.S. Census Bureau, "New Statistics Available from the 2016–2020 American Community Survey 5-Year Estimates," press release CB22-48, March 17, 2022.

U.S. Postal Service, "Postal Facts: 41,704 ZIP Codes," webpage, undated. As of May 7, 2024:
https://facts.usps.com/42000-zip-codes

Wenger, Jennie W., Robert Bozick, Linda Cottrell, and Stephani L. Wrabel, *National Guard Youth ChalleNGe: Program Progress in 2022–2023*, RAND Corporation, RR-A2120-1, 2024. As of May 15, 2024:
https://www.rand.org/pubs/research_reports/RRA2120-1.html

Wenger, Jennie W., Louay Constant, Linda Cottrell, Sy Doan, Daniel Hicks, Jenna W. Kramer, Kata Mihaly, Peter Nguyen, Thomas E. Trail, Stephani L. Wrabel, and Lisa Berdie, *National Guard Youth ChalleNGe: Program Progress in 2020–2021*, RAND Corporation, RR-A1229-1, 2022. As of August 4, 2023:
https://www.rand.org/pubs/research_reports/RRA1229-1.html

Wenger, Jennie W., Louay Constant, Linda Cottrell, Jenna W. Kramer, and Stephani L. Wrabel, *National Guard Youth ChalleNGe: Program Progress in 2019–2020*, RAND Corporation, RR-A882-1, 2021. As of September 1, 2023:
https://www.rand.org/pubs/research_reports/RRA882-1.html

Wenger, Jennie W., Louay Constant, Linda Cottrell, Thomas E. Trail, Michael J. D. Vermeer, and Stephani L. Wrabel, *National Guard Youth ChalleNGe: Program Progress in 2015–2016*, RAND Corporation, RR-1848-OSD, 2017. As of September 20, 2023:
https://www.rand.org/pubs/research_reports/RR1848.html

Wenger, Jennie W., Linda Cottrell, and Stephani L. Wrabel, *National Guard Youth ChalleNGe: Program Progress in 2021–2022*, RAND Corporation, RR-A1229-2, 2023. As of September 1, 2023:
https://www.rand.org/pubs/research_reports/RRA1229-2.html

Wenger, Jennie W., Stephani L. Wrabel, Thomas E. Trail, Louay Constant, Wing Yi Chan, Kathryn A. Edwards, Joy S. Moini, and Hanna Han, *Developing Outcome Measures for the National Guard Youth ChalleNGe Program*, RAND Corporation, RR-A271-5, 2022. As of September 1, 2023:
https://www.rand.org/pubs/research_reports/RRA271-5.html

Wrabel, Stephani L., Jennie W. Wenger, Melissa Kay Diliberti, Christopher Joseph Doss, and Jenna W. Kramer, *Understanding the Impact of Department of Defense Youth Programs on Bridging the Civilian-Military Divide*, RAND Corporation, RR-A2697-1, 2024. As of May 3, 2024:
https://www.rand.org/pubs/research_reports/RRA2697-1.html